SERIES

ARIZONA
HIGHWAYS
They Left Their Mark

Authors:

LEO W. BANKS
JO ANN BROWN
BERNARD L. FONTANA
WILLIAM HAFFORD
AL HEMINGWAY
BJORGNE M. KEITH
DAVID LAVENDER
RON McCOY
DEAN SMITH
JOSEPH STOCKER
TIM VANDERPOOL
KAY JORDAN WHITHAM
LARRY WINTER

Book Editor:
ROBERT J. FARRELL

Design: MARY WINKELMAN VELGOS
Copy Editors: EVELYN HOWELL AND BONNIE SMITH
Research Editor: JEB STUART ROSEBROOK
Production: VICKY SNOW AND ELLEN STRAINE
Front cover art: PHIL BOATWRIGHT
Back cover art: KEVIN KIBSEY

Illustrations and photographs:

COVER   Clockwise from top: Ira Hayes, James Addison Reavis, Zane Grey, Juan Bautista de Anza

PAGE 9   Chief Alchesay. Arizona Historical Foundation

PAGE 21   Juan Bautista de Anza, by Fray Orci, Mexico City, 1774. Museum of New Mexico

PAGE 31   Will Croft Barnes. Arizona Department of Library, Archives, and Public Records

PAGE 49   Dr. George Emery Goodfellow. Arizona Department of Library, Archives, and Public Records

PAGE 55   Zane Grey.

PAGE 65   Jacob Hamblin. Arizona Historical Society

PAGE 71   John Hance. Arizona Historical Society

PAGE 79   Ira Hayes and the Marines raise the American flag over Iwo Jima. Joe Rosenthal, AP/Wide World Photos

PAGE 85   Pete Kitchen. Arizona Historical Society, Tucson

PAGE 113   Sylvester Mowry. California State Library

PAGE 122   James Addison Reavis. Arizona Historical Society, Tucson

PAGE 129   Al Sieber. Sharlot Hall Museum

Prepared by the Book Division of *Arizona Highways*® magazine, a monthly publication of the Arizona Department of Transportation.

Publisher — Nina M. La France
Managing Editor — Bob Albano
Associate Editor — Robert J. Farrell
Art Director — Mary Winkelman Velgos
Production Director — Cindy Mackey

Printed in the United States
Library of Congress Catalog Number 97-727-96
ISBN 0-916179-70-2

S ince Arizona's history first was recorded in the mid-16th century, a number of exceptional individuals have left their mark there. Some, like Juan Bautista de Anza and Sylvester Mowry, played active roles in developing the region. Others, like James Ohio Pattie, J. Ross Browne, and Zane Grey wrote widely read early books about Arizona, their names becoming linked with the place. And yet others, like James Addison Reavis, perpetrated such notorious schemes on Arizona that they are remembered long after their time.

They Left Their Mark gathers 16 stories written by *Arizona Highways* magazine contributors about exceptional individuals whose names are etched in Arizona's history. David Lavender writes about Joseph Rutherford Walker and his explorations; Bernard L. Fontana chronicles the varied life and literary career of Will C. Barnes; Leo W. Banks writes about Al Sieber's courage and Dr. George Emery Goodfellow's unusual medical specialty; the late William Hafford tells of the Apache chief Alchesay; Jo Ann Brown profiles Juan Bautista de Anza's trailblazing; Kay Jordan Whitham writes about naturalist C. Hart Merriam; Larry Winter tells about John Hance's tall tales and Jacob Hamblin's work with the Indians; Al Hemingway writes about World War II hero Ira Hayes; Bjorgne M. Keith tells about land swindler James Addison Reavis; Ron McCoy writes about author J. Ross Browne and pioneer rancher Pete Kitchen; Dean Smith profiles the adventurous James Ohio Pattie; Tim Vanderpool writes about the complex personality of Sylvester Mowry; and Joseph Stocker examines Zane Grey and his time in Arizona.

CHAPTER ONE

Alchesay

*A highly respected chief of the White Mountain
Apache Indians, Alchesay led his people
in battle and in peace. As a scout he was
instrumental in the surrender of Geronimo and
earned a Congressional Medal of Honor. But in
his role of guiding his tribe successfully into the
20th century, he was even more impressive.*

BY WILLIAM HAFFORD

≡>•<≡

S OME YEARS AGO, A DEVOTEE OF MILITARY HISTORY WAS shocked when he learned that the remains of a Congressional Medal of Honor recipient were buried in an unmarked grave in a remote and rugged area of Arizona's White Mountain country. The man's well-intentioned plan was to find the exact location, dig up the remains, and ship them east to Arlington National Cemetery.

But he never executed his plan as he no doubt found that this Medal of Honor recipient is enjoying his final rest at the exact spot he requested. Interred there is Alchesay, the most revered of all the hereditary chiefs of the White Mountain Apache Tribe. The burial site, surrounded by 2,500 square miles of the deep canyons and pine forests of the Fort Apache Indian Reservation, was chosen by Alchesay himself prior to his passing. And he was laid to rest according to the rituals and traditions of his people. The piñon tree is his living headstone.

Although he could neither read nor write, Alchesay's correspondence with high federal officials (dictated and signed with his thumb print) reflects a high native intelligence and an astute grasp of politics and the future. He was an active proponent of education and advocated self-sufficiency for his people.

During frontier campaigns against Geronimo and other Apache factions hostile to the U.S. government, Alchesay served in the U.S. Army as a sergeant of scouts. He frequently rode at the side of General George Crook, who considered him a valued advisor. And on the field of battle, his valor was such that he was awarded the nation's highest military tribute, the Congressional Medal of Honor.

From earliest manhood, Alchesay understood that white settlers would continue their westward migration in ever-increasing numbers. He envisioned a prosperous future for his people only if they learned to live cooperatively with the whites. He understood, also, that Apache warriors, while holding a well-earned reputation as masters of guerrilla warfare, could never prevail on a long-term basis against the overwhelming might of the U.S. military.

Alchesay's perspective on the future, as well as his techniques of tribal leadership, he learned from his uncle, Chief Pedro. Pedro, leader of the White Mountain Apache (more specifically "the red rock strata clan"), was a wily old diplomat who had maintained good relationships with the American military for many years. Comparing the White Mountain Apache people with Geronimo and his followers would be like comparing Iowa farmers with Al Capone. In fact, many peaceful Apache people of the Geronimo era were as fearful of the rampaging Geronimo and his followers (mostly Chiricahua Apaches) as were white settlers. For example, in November, 1885, a renegade band attacked Apache villages on the reservation, killing 12 and carrying away six women and children. And for nearly a year in the late 1880s, peaceful Apaches were afraid to hunt on their own land because of frequent bloody assaults by the renegades.

For many years, Pedro's people had wandered a wide area in the rather inhospitable region near Mount Turnbull, south of today's San Carlos Lake. But about 1850, Pedro, in an agreement with Diablo (leader of the powerful "slender peak standing up" clan) obtained a large permanent tract of land in the high mountain country near the present-day community of Whiteriver. Sometime around 1853, Alchesay was born near Limestone Creek. His mother was Pedro's sister.

When he was a youngster, Alchesay's energy and quick mind caught Pedro's attention. The aging chief marked his handsome nephew for a leadership role at an early age. In his teens Alchesay became Pedro's subchief.

When Gen. George Crook arrived in Arizona in 1871, Alchesay's responsibilities to his people took a sudden and unexpected turn. Crook, routinely considered the greatest Indian fighter in U.S. military history, knew that his troops could never subdue (or in most cases even locate) the marauding Apache bands that insisted on bloodshed and pillaging. Said Crook, "We must use Apache methods and Apache soldiers."

Crook met with the White Mountain Apache leaders, winning the trust of old Pedro, Miguel, Diablo, and the young subchiefs Alchesay and Petone. History confirms that the peaceful Apaches' impression of Crook was correct. The bearded general, while merciless in combat with rebellious

Apaches, relentlessly repeated his conviction (to Washington bureaucrats and frontier settlers alike) that the peaceful Apache should be treated as equals in all matters.

The tribal leaders were unanimous in their agreement to permit and encourage their young men to enlist as U.S. Army scouts. Alchesay himself set the example by joining up. His army record provides the following information: Date of enlistment — December 2, 1872. Age — 20.

Height — 6 feet 1 inch. Complexion — copper. Hair — black.

Alchesay was a man who stood out in any crowd. With jutting cheekbones, an aquiline nose, and full lips, he looked like a scout sent from Hollywood's central casting. And he dressed as though he had stepped from the pages of an Indian version of *Gentlemen's Quarterly.* Photos show him standing half-a-head, or more, above most of the white troopers, wearing conventional trousers and shirt, but also the traditional Apache loin cloth, high leather moccasins, native jewelry, and a bandoleer of cartridges. His long, black hair was either wrapped with a colorful scarf or kept under a broad-brimmed hat.

Apache scouts like Alchesay were the frontier equivalent of today's Green Berets. Capt. John G. Bourke, in his book *On the Border With Crook,* states that in the entire campaign to subjugate Geronimo not a single outlaw Apache was killed, wounded, or captured by white troops. While Crook and his men provided the strategy and support, it was the Apache scouts who engaged the hostiles and brought frontier bloodshed to an early end.

Said one white officer of his scouts: "No one else can follow a trail as they can, and no one else can stand so much fatigue. My scouts will start at the bottom of a 1,500-foot mountain, and go on a trot clear to the top without stopping. There isn't a white man alive who could run 50 yards up a slope like that without stopping to catch his wind."

It was during General Crook's winter campaign of 1872-73 that Alchesay earned his Congressional Medal of Honor. Until World War I, citations for the medal were extremely brief and did not profile specific acts of bravery.

But, surely, Alchesay's performance at the Battle of Turret Mountain would be typical of his battlefield performance.

In late March, 1873, the Apache scouts, accompanied by white Army troops, were looking for an outlaw band of Tonto Apaches that had tortured and killed three settlers near Wickenburg. Alchesay and his scouts were put on the trail, but locating the ruthless gang was no easy task. Finally, the scouts captured a Tonto Apache woman who revealed the location of the hostiles. On March 27, Alchesay led his scouts to the top of Turret Mountain where the outlaws were hiding and, in a lightning pre-dawn attack, killed more than 50 and captured 15.

Similar engagements throughout central Arizona diminished the threat to frontier settlers. In April, Alchesay and his scouts located the hidden camp of Deltchay (leader of the last major band of renegades in the region). The scouts surprised them with a deadly barrage, and the initial phase of Crook's Apache campaign was essentially over. Alchesay was recommended for the Medal of Honor as were other scouts. When awarded in 1875, Alchesay's citation said simply, "for gallant conduct during campaigns against Apaches during the winter of 1872-1873."

Alchesay was honorably discharged in February of 1874, but was called back into service that August. Alchesay and 30 scouts, accompanied by a white officer, chased a band of renegades under Chappo and literally wiped out the outlaws. These mopping-up expeditions continued until the spring of 1875 when virtually no hostile bands of any consequence remained. The Army transferred General Crook to the Department of the Platte and again discharged Alchesay and his scouts from service.

In Crook's absence, the plight of the Apache took a slow but inexorable turn for the worse under the corrupt administration of the new Indian Agent Joseph C. Tiffany. Through fraud and theft of the Apaches' food and clothing rations, Tiffany nearly starved and froze to death the peaceful reservation Indians.

In late summer of 1881, Tiffany had Alchesay and 10 prominent members of Pedro's clan arrested for the murder of a government scout. They were jailed in the Fort Apache guardhouse, then transferred to the jail at Fort Thomas, where they were held by Agent Tiffany for 14 months without any charges being filed against them. Evidence indicated that neither Alchesay or any member of his group had anything to do with the crime. Even in the face of a government order to either try the men or release them, Tiffany continued to hold them.

Finally, an anonymous individual (or perhaps a group) hired a Tucson law firm to assist Alchesay and the others. A Tucson newspaper took up the cause, and, eventually, a federal grand jury was seated. The grand jury released the Apaches with some harsh words for Agent Tiffany: "How any official possessing the slightest manhood would keep 11 men in confinement for 14 months without charges, knowing them to be innocent, is a total mystery." Shortly thereafter Tiffany, fired from his position, slithered off into obscurity.

Many noticed that Alchesay, after his release, never displayed the slightest bitterness or resentment against the white community. He continued as a leader of his people and worked cooperatively with government officials. Said one of his white friends, "Without saying a word, he showed us all how to accept the difficulties of a difficult world."

In 1882 Crook returned to Arizona and was shocked at the deterioration that had occurred during his absence. The incensed officer took firm measures to correct the situation, then turned his attention to the matter of Geronimo and the wild-running Chiricahuas who were operating almost exclusively out of the Sierra Madres in northern Mexico. Alchesay again offered his services to General Crook and served primarily as an advisor to the general over the next several years,.

On the night of March 25, 1886, Alchesay carried out his last, and perhaps most dangerous, military assignment. Geronimo had agreed to a meeting with General Crook near the Mexican border. The conditions of the meeting, stipulated by Geronimo, gave the renegades a distinct military advantage. After dark, Crook asked Alchesay if he would be willing to go into Geronimo's camp and try to negotiate a surrender. Alchesay, with Apache scout Kae-tenna at his shoulder, went.

During the final stages of his bloody career, Geronimo was often in a state of high-voltage paranoia made worse by his conspicuous consumption of alcohol. The same could be said of subchief Naiche and others. Throughout the night, Alchesay talked with the exhausted, mostly drunk renegades — all of whom were armed to the teeth. The next day, Geronimo agreed to surrender, and Crook credited Alchesay and his companion scout. "Without their aid, surrender could not have been achieved," he said.

But Geronimo's surrender was short-lived. A notorious whiskey peddler, named Bob Tribollet, slipped into Geronimo's encampment and sold the old medicine man a new supply of rotgut. Fortified by alcohol, Geronimo and about 20 warriors fled into the night. The majority of the renegades returned peacefully to the reservation. It took five more months of hide-and-seek in the borderlands before a bedraggled Geronimo finally threw in the towel.

In the atmosphere of peace that followed, Alchesay raised cattle, continued to deal effectively with government officials, and was instrumental in bringing a large boarding school to the reservation. He also made lasting friendships with many whites.

Perhaps the strongest of these friendships was with the Rev. Edgar Guenther, a Lutheran minister who arrived on the Fort Apache Reservation in 1912. Alchesay obtained land for the new minister's church, and, thereafter, a warm relationship developed. The two men hiked the mountain country, hunted and socialized together, and worked as a team to further the interest of the Apache people.

The minister's son, Arthur Alchesay Guenther (namesake of the chief and today minister of that original church), remembers incidents from that rich association. Recalls the younger Guenther, "A terrible flu epidemic hit about 1919. My father was working himself to the bone, traveling the reservation and trying to help the sick. He exhausted himself to the point of collapse, and this was noticed by Alchesay. The chief urged him to rest, but Dad just kept going. Finally, Alchesay exercised his tribal authority, and with the forceful demeanor of a great chief, officially banished my father from the reservation. He and my mother went to Oceanside, California, and stayed there until my father's health returned."

On another occasion, the barn behind the Guenther home burned down. Inside was the senior Guenther's first automobile, a new Model-T. In collusion with Agency

Superintendent Davis, Alchesay persuaded the minister to join them on a fishing trip for a few days — a short sojourn to take his mind off the unfortunate event. "While they were gone," says the younger Guenther, "wagon loads of Apache people arrived at the church. Lumber was hauled over from the tribal sawmill, and by the time the fishing party returned, a new barn, freshly painted, was standing at the site of the fire."

The Lutheran church, near the center of the community of Whiteriver, was completed and ready for its first service on April 30, 1922. Alchesay and Apache people from all over the reservation arrived for the dedication ceremony. Alchesay was given permanent possession of a key to the church, and it was he who officially opened its door and, during that first service, delivered a brief but touching talk to the white and Indian congregation.

The younger Guenther knew Alchesay only in his earliest years when the old chief was beyond 70. "I remember him riding into town on his horse, sitting very tall. The kids would run alongside, each hoping to be the one that would get to take the reins and tie the animal. He took me horseback riding many times. Sometimes, he took me for walks, always holding my hand. 'Way back when General Crook came to the reservation, the government assigned identification numbers (much like Social Security numbers) to the people. Alchesay got the first number, A-1. When I was a kid, and because I was named after him, my nickname was A-1." (A-1 Lake, atop the Mogollon Rim, also is named for Alchesay.)

"When Alchesay was in his last days, I remember going with my mother and father up to his ranch to deliver soup," recalled the younger Guenther. "He died in the late summer of 1928. My father was away from the reservation at the time. A young minister named Paul Behne conducted services in the church. Then the Apache people transported his body to his chosen burial site in the area of Little Round Top Peak. Being small, and since my father was away, I wasn't able to go up there."

Lois Wilson, member of a White Mountain ranching family, recalls that she and her parents were the only white people present at the actual burial. "I was a small child at the time. Alchesay was carried to the burial site on his favorite horse. All of his personal belongings were buried with him. Other belongings not buried with him were burned."

Many years later, Alchesay's daughter, Bertha, told the Guenther family that the key to the White River church went into the grave with her father. "When he was dying," Bertha said, "he asked that the key be placed in his hand and buried with him. We did that."

The piñon pine that marks the grave was only a sapling at the time of Alchesay's interment. Today the tree has a trunk nearly a foot-and-a-half in diameter. It grows in the red soil of a nearly hidden canyon. Do not ask its exact location. Unless you are a White Mountain Apache, you have no need to know.

CHAPTER TWO

Juan Bautista de Anza

*Born the son of a presidio commander
on the frontier of northern Mexico,
Juan Bautista de Anza grew up as a
successful military man. But his lasting fame
came from leading civilian Spanish settlers
to open the route from Tubac, Arizona,
to the San Francisco Bay.*

BY JO ANN BROWN

J UAN BAUTISTA DE ANZA — THE 18TH-CENTURY MILITARY
man, pathfinder, and peacemaker for the Spanish
empire — left his mark deep and wide across the borderlands of Arizona, northern Mexico, New Mexico, and
California. Consider some of the accomplishments of his
52 years:

•Thirty years before the Lewis and Clark expedition,
Anza opened the first overland route to the Pacific Coast,
linking Spain's isolated outposts in California with her settlements and supply routes to the southeast.

•He then recruited and led 240 people, including
many women and children, through Sonora and southern
Arizona to Monterey. A number of these families later settled in the San Francisco Bay area.

•As a military commander, Anza fought hand-to-hand
against unfriendly tribes and participated in high-level
councils of war. He oversaw the fair treatment of his men,

defended peaceable Indians and settlers, and regulated a host of domestic matters ranging from irrigation rights to cattle brands.

•As provincial governor of New Mexico, Anza saved the Hopis from starvation, blazed a trade route from Santa Fe to Sonora, ruptured an alliance between the Navajo and Gila Apache who were attacking Spanish settlements, and made peace with the western Comanche after brilliantly routing their fearsome leader Cuerno Verde (Spanish for "green horn").

•By his own account, he participated in more than a hundred battles, killed 173 enemies, took 612 prisoners, and suffered three major wounds. He logged more than 12,000 miles in exploration-related travel, but the "constant violent" exercise of riding a horse in his military commands wore him out even more, resulting in the dislocation of both feet and chronic discomfort.

Born in 1736 to the presidio commander at Fronteras (about 35 miles south of Douglas, Arizona), Anza was named both for his father and for his Basque grandfather, who had commanded the Janos presidio (south of today's Deming, New Mexico) after emigrating from Spain. Apaches ambushed and killed young Anza's father in 1740.

In 1752 he began his career as a volunteer at the Fronteras presidio. Three years later he became a lieutenant. After several long forays against the Apaches, Anza was promoted to captain of the Tubac presidio, south of today's Tucson.

Early in this command, a Jesuit missionary sang his praises: "Legitimate son of his father . . . he inherited with the name . . . a solid disposition, valor, rapport with his soldiers, and the ability to place himself on their level and to excel them in bearing the hardships and the duties as well as the good fortune of the expeditions."

The eminent Marques de Rubi inspected the Tubac presidio in December, 1766, and noted that, unlike other commanders, Anza supplied his men with armor-like leather jackets and other necessities at discounted prices. Rubi concluded that Anza was "because of his energy, valor, zeal, intelligence, and notable disinterestedness, a complete officer" and worthy of royal favor.

Like his father many years earlier, Anza dreamed of exploring the land beyond the Colorado River. By 1772 the time was right — Spain feared a Russian or English invasion of California. To avert such a menace, Governor Gaspar de Portola of Baja California and a small contingent had marched north from San Diego and scouted the Monterey area in 1769. Local Indians, spotting these "white men with long clothing," had spread the news eastward. Anza got wind of it in Tubac, and promptly requested permission to open a route between Sonora and Monterey.

Viceroy Antonio Maria Bucareli approved. The handful of men remaining at Monterey needed supplies and settlers, and sea travel from Baja had proven extremely risky. Anza gathered experienced soldiers and muleteers as well as all manner of provisions — food, tools, and gifts to smooth the way through the lands of the Pima, Papago, Yuma, and Californian tribes. Weapons and ammunition were allowed, but only for self-defense.

The expedition left Tubac on January 8, 1774, and a month later reached Yuman settlements along the Colorado River. Anza noted the "great guilelessness and friendship" of these handsome half-naked people who sported elaborate coiffures and body paint. He presented one of their chiefs (dubbed Salvador Palma) with a shiny beribboned likeness of Carlos II, "confirming him in his office, that he might rule legally and with greater authority, and be recognized even by the Spaniards, who would respect his rights."

Won over, the Yumas helped the party cross the Colorado by carrying much of the baggage as well as the supine body of non-swimming Father Francisco Garces, one of the expedition's chaplains.

Anza reached Monterey on April 8, 1774. Upon reporting to Viceroy Bucareli in Mexico City later that year, Anza stressed the need for skillful diplomacy with the Yumas, upon whose cooperation any successful Colorado River crossing depended.

Bucareli agreed, promoted Anza to lieutenant colonel, and ordered him to recruit, equip, and shepherd 30 families to settle near San Francisco Bay. Again Anza delivered. He rode northwest from Mexico City to the coastal towns of Sinaloa and Sonora, where he found people desperate enough to gamble everything on a fresh start in an unknown land. Then he invested in cattle, clothing, and all manner of supplies, down to petticoats and ribbons for the women.

The expedition left Tubac on October 23, 1775. Fifteen miles north of the presidio a mother died in childbirth. After her burial at San Xavier del Bac, three couples from the party married. The expedition pushed on.

At the Colorado River the Yumas waited, this time fully clothed. Anza found their desire for conversion to the Catholic faith touching: "One of many proofs [of their sincerity] is that now when they show us their wives they boast that they have only one. Another is that they still know how to say 'Ave Maria'. . . ."

Anza assured the Indians that in due time missionaries and aid would arrive. Enthused, many waded into the muddy currents of the Colorado with the travelers, some guiding horses and others flanking riders. Three tribesmen again carried Father Garces across.

Increased by two more births, the expedition reached Monterey on March 10, 1776. Anza turned over his charges to Lt. José Joaquin Moraga, then scouted the San Francisco Bay area for suitable locations for a presidio and settlement. He returned to Monterey to say farewell: "When I mounted my horse in the plaza, the people whom I had led from their fatherlands . . . especially the female sex, came to me sobbing with tears, which they declared they were shedding more because of my departure than of their exile, filling me with compassion. They showered me with embraces, best wishes, and praises which I do not merit." Anza and a small party freighted 19 mule loads of supplies to the outposts of southern California, including a cage of cats for the mouse-ridden missions of San Gabriel and San Diego, then turned east.

Spring flooding had made the Colorado River impossible to cross without the Yumas' ferrying assistance. Hoping to ensure continued good relations, Anza persuaded Palma and several companions to journey on with him to Mexico City, where he presented the tribesmen to Viceroy Bucareli and stood as Palma's baptismal godfather. The Indians left for home dazzled by the prospect of life as Spanish subjects, their ears ringing with promises of commerce, missionaries, and military protection. Little did they expect a long delay caused in part by a new administration.

To boost defenses between Texas and the Californias from Apaches, Seris, and other warlike tribes, the crown severed this region from Bucareli's viceroyalty and called it the Internal Provinces of New Spain, selecting as its capital the remote Sonoran town of Arizpe. A commander named Teodoro de Croix took charge. Strapped by a tight budget and harried by widespread Indian depredations, Croix gave low priority to the Yumas. Rather than sending Anza back to their territory, Croix ordered him to put down a Seri rebellion in Sonora and later released him to carry out a royal appointment as governor of New Mexico. Anza had no further contact with the Yumas.

For two years, the tribe waited for the Spanish and their goods. Father Garces and two soldiers arrived in August, 1779, with tobacco, cloth, and trinkets, but the Yumas, having been promised much, expected more. Croix got around to commissioning the promised developments in 1780, but by then the tribe had grown disillusioned. To make matters worse, Croix pinched pennies by funding two makeshift mission-presidial centers, each to anchor a small white population planted hundreds of miles from the nearest Spanish outpost.

Settlers arrived with few gifts for their native hosts but built their houses and grazed their horses and livestock upon tribal croplands. Rebellious Yumas got a taste of another Spanish import, the whipping post. On July 17, 1781, the Indians vented their accumulated frustrations by pillaging the settlements and clubbing to death their commander. For two more days they rampaged, killing 104 people (including Father Garces) and taking hostage many women and children.

Spanish forces later regained the captives and some of the bodies, but not the goodwill of the Yumas. Spain's settlements in California sank back into isolation. Although Anza and Garces had often warned against such a scenario, Croix spread the notion that the pair had misled him.

By this time, Anza had gone a long way toward ending tribal unrest along the New Mexican frontier, but had angered some of his own countrymen by moving them from their scattered ranches into defensible towns. Protesters swarmed to Arizpe in 1780. As a result, Croix ordered Anza to stop consolidating settlers in the Santa Fe area, but allowed him to go ahead with a similar plan to cluster missionaries. Soon Croix left the Internal Provinces to become Viceroy of Peru.

Croix's successor was the recent governor of California, Felipe de Neve, a man deeply embittered by the Yuma massacre and resentful of Anza, perhaps because of Croix's allegations. Barely had Neve taken over when another band of New Mexicans descended on Arizpe to protest Anza's resettlement efforts. Without hearing Anza's side, Neve accused him of bad management and ordered him to drop from his service record claims of having opened the route to California and of having defeated Cuerno Verde. Then he sought to replace him as governor.

Neve died in 1784. Anza rebutted his charges and the

royal council revoked Neve's action on the service record, but Anza wanted out of New Mexico. He hated Santa Fe's cold winters and believed that his health was failing. He also had a wife and two orphaned nieces to think about. In December, 1786, he petitioned Carlos III for lighter duty.

The next year he got it. Fernando de la Concha took over for him as governor in August, 1787, and Anza headed for Sonora as commander of arms. Soon he was also named captain of Tucson. At last, in 1788, the crown granted Anza a position befitting his experience and colonelcy — service in Spain.

He did not live long enough to go. On December 19, 1788, Anza collapsed and died in Arizpe. He was buried the next day under the floor of the local church, Nuestra Señora de la Asuncion. A short entry in the parish burial register recorded the general location of his grave. His widow, Ana Maria Perez Serrano, inherited his estate, which included land in Sonora as well as ranches near Tubac and Sasabe. As the years passed and Spain lost control of the Internal Provinces, the memory of Anza faded and by the late 19th century, he was virtually unknown.

The discovery early this century of his California expedition journals restored Anza to public awareness and delighted historians. Alfred Barnaby Thomas, in *Forgotten Frontiers*, the 1932 study of Anza's governorship of New Mexico, ranked Anza with Daniel Boone and Kit Carson. Noted borderlands historian Herbert E. Bolton, who translated, edited, and published the journals, hit the road between Sonora and Monterey to test their accuracy. Anza's dry but detailed entries meshed with the other documents, and Bolton exulted in 1931, ". . . I have been able to identify practically every water hole and camp site."

And while Anza's journals brought well-deserved recognition for his ability as the explorer who led a remarkable cross-country expedition to northern California, they also inspired the *San Francisco Chronicle* in 1903 to erroneously promote him as the municipal founding father, even though he only explored the area around the bay.

Bolton and other historians later clarified Anza's role in the development of the San Francisco Bay area, but the myth persisted. In 1961 it inspired the pastor of the Nuestra Señora de la Asuncion church and the Arizpe city council to seek financial help from the city of San Francisco in replacing the worn-out pine floor of the church: "in light of the certainty that in this church rest the remains of the Cavalier de Anza, the founder of the city of San Francisco . . . ."

A flurry of correspondence followed. Result: The University of California donated a generous sum for a new oak floor and sent archaeologist Dr. Robert F. Heizer, physical anthropologist Dr. T.D. McCown, and geologist Dr. Howel Williams to Arizpe on February 21, 1963, with instructions to witness the excavation and, if possible, to identify Anza's remains. There was just one problem — the pertinent page in the burial register was missing.

Having no idea of the exact location of Anza's grave, the excavators relied on the tradition that important secular people had been buried in the nave and began digging in that section on February 23. Soon they unearthed many burials, including a coffined skeleton dressed in a military uniform from the late 18th century. Dr. McCown, who had identified the remains of California missionary Father Junipero Serra in 1943, examined and measured the bones, comparing them with the little information known about

Anza's stature and physical condition at the time of his death.

Finding no evidence to the contrary, the team ruled that the remains were indeed those of Juan Bautista de Anza. Two months later, the Instituto Nacional de Antropologia e Historia of Mexico City conducted an independent investigation and reached the same conclusion. Dr. Arthur Woodward, an Arizona authority on historic costume, concurred.

The reported discovery in 1963 of what were thought to be Anza's remains beneath a church floor in Sonora caused a sensation on both sides of the border. Because of the intense media attention, the parish scrapped plans for a simple reinterment and hosted an elaborate international ceremony on May 30, 1963, in which the skeleton was laid to rest in a marble sarcophagus set in a tile floor.

But 13 years later, Sonora Director of Tourism Dr. Sergio Bribiesca Elvira discovered the register page with Anza's burial entry. To the embarrassment of many, it revealed that Anza had been interred nowhere near the nave, but in a side chapel. The skeleton mistaken for Anza's may be that of Manuel de Echeagaray, another late-18th-century Sonoran military commander. Opinions differ as to what, if anything, should be done.

What Anza himself would want done is not clear. Anza understood human nature better than most of his peers. He scandalized Father Pedro Font, chaplain and cosmographer of the second California expedition, on Christmas Eve, 1775, by rationing a pint of brandy to each adult traveler; and he aggravated the dour priest on another occasion by defending a "very bold widow" from being beaten by her jealous boyfriend. Throughout his career, Anza showed mercy to the less fortunate. For these reasons, he might want his countrymen spared the pain and expense of altering the church.

On the other hand, his contemporaries sometimes accused him of grandstanding. Father Garces grumbled in 1775 that Anza "says something different in different company." Father Pedro Font sarcastically referred to Anza in his diary as an "absolute lord" who wanted "all the glory for himself." No doubt the attention would please him, as would other tributes, including the Sociedad Sonorense de Historia and the Tubac Presidio State Historic Park honoring the bicentennial of his death in 1988, the establishment of the vast Anza-Borrego Desert State Park in southern California, and the display of his likeness atop a dashing equestrian statue in Hermosillo, Sonora.

Anza would indeed be pleased that an imposing commemorative plaque outside the church does not credit him with founding San Francisco. As ambitious as he may have been, and as proud of his accomplishments as he was, Anza never claimed such an honor.

CHAPTER THREE

William Croft Barnes

Best known for his book Arizona Place Names,
*Will C. Barnes led a remarkable and varied life
that included stints as an Indian fighter
and a bureaucrat and that spanned the country
from Arizona to Washington, D.C.*

BY BERNARD L. FONTANA

———◆———

SOLDIER, RANCHER, POLITICIAN, FORESTER, CONSERVATION-ist, historian, folklorist, devoted husband, and writer. Each describes Will C. Barnes, a man whose 5 foot 4 inch stature cast an uncommonly long shadow on his adopted Arizona and, indeed, on the American West.

Little that happened in the first two decades of his life suggested what the remaining years would hold. Born in San Francisco, California, on June 21, 1858, Will Barnes spent his earliest years in a Nevada mining camp, later moving to Indiana, Minnesota, Indiana once again, and then San Francisco once more, where he met an Army signalman who sold him on the idea of a career in the Army Signal Corps.

In 1879 at age 21, Private Barnes found himself learning basic meteorology and signaling, including telegraphy, at the signal school, at today's Fort Myer, Virginia. He finished his course as a telegrapher and assistant weather observer and, before the year was out, received orders to report to Fort Apache in the heart of

Apache country, high in Arizona's White Mountains area.

The trip to Fort Apache from San Diego was by train to Casa Grande, Arizona, then by stagecoach to Tucson and on to the White Mountains. Barnes arrived in Tucson in February, 1880. "In the midst of a cloud of dust . . . ," he penned in his diary.

> The place seemed lively enough. Having hunted up the Telegraph office and made myself known I found that I would have to wait nearly a week for the next stage. I soon exhausted the town as it was such a horrible little place and every house just like its neighbor, one story dobe [*sic*] . . . . I at last find myself on the top of a fine coach with six dashing mustangs at the bit pulling out of Tucson on a bright but rather chilly morning [headed for Fort Apache].

In *Apaches & Longhorns*, his autobiography published many years later, Barnes elaborated his unflattering description of Tucson. "To the tenderfoot," he wrote, "the town was a constant source of amusement and amazement."

> The hotel office was in the large bar-room, the only room that boasted a board floor. This room was full of rough-looking men who were patronizing the bar in great style. Soft drinks were then unknown. It was "whiskey straight," or, perhaps, a shot of Mexican mescal . . . .
> . . . It seemed that every other building on the business street was a saloon — every one packed with a motley crowd of men of many

nationalities . . . . Nearly everyone was armed
. . . [and] used the Spanish language. In each
place a number of gambling games ran steadily
. . . . Everyone was either struggling to reach
the bar for a drink or . . . one of the games.

The intermediate buildings along the
street were occupied by *nymphs de pavé* of every
race and color . . . . The two classes of business,
gambling and prostitution, were evidently on a
par as to respectability with the selling of dry-
goods and grocers.

With Tucson behind him, Barnes started the long
stage trip to Fort Apache, riding there via Fort Thomas.
The 90-mile stretch between forts Thomas and Apache was
covered by a pack train of 40 mules carrying guns and
ammunition as well as Barnes' zinc-covered Saratoga
trunk. At a spot called Ash Fork, the troops were attacked
by Apaches. "Can you imagine the thrill I was getting? My
first Indian fight! What a joyful experience!" Barnes exulted in his autobiography.

With no casualties on either side, the pack train
escaped the Apache attack under cover of darkness and
proceeded to Fort Apache. It was, observed Barnes, "in
those days a beautiful spot. The forests around it were full
of wild game . . . . Every stream in the mountains was full
of the finest trout that ever swam in cold water. It was,
indeed a sportsman's paradise."

In 1881 trouble brewed for Barnes and his fellow
soldiers. An Apache medicine man named Nock-aye-det-
klin-ne initiated what anthropologists have since labeled a
"revitalization movement." By 1881 Western Apaches had

come to feel the weight of their American oppressors, and early in that year Nock-aye-det-klin-ne professed to his fellow tribesmen he could raise the dead and commune with spirits. He predicted whites would be driven from Apache lands.

All of this frightened the Indian agent, who called on Col. E.A. Carr, commanding officer at Fort Apache, to "arrest or kill him, or both." Subsequently, Carr led more than 70 white troops and a smaller contingent of Apache scouts to arrest the medicine man at his camp on Cibecue Creek. The surrender had been peaceful, but as the soldiers made camp for the night, others of the Indians shot and killed Capt. Edmund C. Hentig. During the ensuing melee, the Apache scouts deserted, some of them to fight on the side of their own people. In addition to Hentig, Nock-aye-det-klin-ne and seven soldiers died as a result of the encounter.

There were tense hours of anticipation back at Fort Apache while the few troops who had remained there awaited word of what had happened. Barnes, who had not gone to Cibecue, manned an observation post alone in sight of threatening Apaches until Carr and his men returned. And a few days later Barnes and a civilian scout volunteered to carry messages to Fort Thomas to seek relief for the beleaguered soldiers at Fort Apache. For these actions he was awarded the Congressional Medal of Honor in 1883, by which time he had been promoted to sergeant.

While still in the Army, the signalman became cattle-man, buying into a ranch north of Fort Apache near Holbrook with some partners. Barnes was given an early military discharge because of problems with his eyes, and in 1884 the 25-year-old rancher bought his partners out and began raising cattle while making political hay. He was appointed to an important regulating agency, the Arizona Livestock Sanitary Board, in 1887, serving on it most of the time until 1900. In 1892 he successfully ran as a Republican for county commissioner of Apache County, and in 1894 he was elected to the 18th Territorial Legislative Assembly.

When he was 39, in 1897, Will Barnes married Edith Talbot, daughter of Walter Talbot, a prominent Phoenix merchant who became that city's mayor in 1900. Always a "we," they were partners in many ventures and remained the closest of friends until death eventually parted them.

In 1900 Will and Edith moved their ranching opera-tion to New Mexico. During their first half-dozen years there, Will served in the territorial legislature (1901-02), on the territory's Livestock Sanitary Board (1902-06), and as secretary of the New Mexico Cattle Growers' Association.

In 1906, having suffered drought and cruel winters, the Barnes' gave up ranching. But a year later, having been persuaded by Gifford Pinchot to accept the job, Will became an inspector of grazing in the national forests, turning his attention for the next 21 years to the preserva-tion of our nation's forests and public rangelands. He lived most of this time in Washington, D.C., working there in the Department of Agriculture's Division of Forestry.

Conservationist Barnes helped institute a system of permits to cut trees in national forests. He mediated between sheep men and those pressing for the preservation of wild game. And he received congressional approval to help save longhorn cattle from extinction by selecting a small herd of them to graze in Oklahoma's Wichita National Forest where the breed has been perpetuated.

Many old-time cattlemen who recalled the days of open ranges were less than enthusiastic about ever-increasing controls forced on them by the Forest Service. Barnes, though, was always ready to answer critics. He replied to one of them in 1927:

> When I came into the Forest Service the stockmen did not know from year to year where they were going to land. The ranges were over-stocked, we were all fighting for grass, our cattle were dying, cattle thieves were robbing us day and night, prices were low, and the business was in bad shape. When I go back to my old range in Arizona I find everybody contented, no fights, no troubles, every man has his own range, and they are all fairly prosperous in spite of talk to the contrary. There was as much grass on the Forests in northern Arizona this last year as I can remember seeing since the days when the first cattle occupied them. I went over every National Forest in the state this summer [and] compared them with the old time conditions, and I felt that the Forest Service had made good.

After his retirement from the Forest Service in 1929, Barnes was made paid secretary of the United States Geographic Board, a body on which he had served without pay since 1920. It was that involvement perhaps more than any other which led him eventually to write the book for which he remains best known in his adopted state, *Arizona Place Names*. By the time his finest work was finished, he had long been a published author. His first article, about Apaches, was published in *Youth's Companion* in 1885. His many pieces, both semi-fictional cowboy tales and factual pieces on grazing and conservation matters, were published in such journals as *Overland Monthly*, *McClure's Magazine*, *Out West*, *Harper's Weekly*, *Pacific Monthly*, *The Cosmopolitan*, *Atlantic Monthly*, and others. And with William MacLeod Raine, he had written *Cattle* (1930), an important book on the range cattle industry, with much in it about Arizona.

In 1932 Barnes wrote the Macmillan Company as a potential publisher for his next book:

> For almost 40 years I have been gathering items on the origin and meaning of Arizona place names. The matter has always intrigued me and through a habit of setting down the statements of old timers and others I have accumulated a list of over 4,000 separate names.
> Not only have I given the origin and meaning of each — as far as that could be discovered but have also made the material historically valuable by giving a short snappy [sic]account of its historical origin.

> I have put in a lot of hard work on this ms [manuscript] and feel that it is just about as near correct as human intelligence can make it.

Because he relied almost entirely on non-Indian and non-Hispanic informants, the Indian and Spanish place names in Barnes' book leave a great deal to be desired. So is it weak on southern Arizona, but his "short snappy" accounts and his having lived on the ground at a time when Anglo place names were daily being applied to the land give his book, first published by the University of Arizona in 1935, a unique immediacy. To paraphrase one early reviewer, I leave it to others to argue over the book's bones while I savor the meat.

Will Barnes died in Phoenix in December, 1936. Earlier, from 1934 to 1936, *Arizona Highways* published 11 of his articles. And in 1941, his well-told autobiography, *Apaches & Longhorns*, was published posthumously by the Ward Ritchie Press. It was reissued by the University of Arizona Press in 1982.

Barnes' physical remains lie buried in Arlington National Cemetery. But his literary remains, like his legacy of conservation in the national forests, continue alive and well among the descendants of Americans whom he served faithfully. His is an honored place in the roster of Arizona names.

John Ross Browne

*Recounting his "rambles" in Arizona
in the mid-1860s, J. Ross Browne was among
the first to write about the region. His often
witty observations about the frontier settlers,
clashes with the Indians, and descriptions
of the riches of the region painted an image
of Arizona in the minds of the American
public that lasted nearly a century.*

B Y   R O N   M C C O Y

———❖———

I N 1864 JOHN ROSS BROWNE ENJOYED FAME AS THE author-illustrator of acerbically witty, widely read books and articles about his many adventures. His accurate descriptions of exotic places and people, often interspersed with droll, self-deprecating humor, informed and charmed his readers. What he called his "rambles" included sailing on a whaling ship to Zanzibar, crossing the Isthmus of Panama, steaming up the Pacific Coast to Alaska, and exploring the gold fields of California and Nevada. But while those trips carried a certain amount of adventure, his trip to Arizona Territory, he later confided to his wife, had truly been "an enterprise of considerable hazard."

Going to Arizona took the 43-year-old, Irish-born Browne to a place possessing a "peculiar charm in the absence of accommodation for travelers, and extraordinary advantages in the way of burning deserts, dried rivers, rattlesnakes, [and] scorpions . . . besides unlimited fascinations in the line of robbery, starvation, and the chances of sudden death by accident." The 4,500 or so American citizens living in Arizona had been devastated by incessant Apache warfare and had neither telegraph nor railroad to the outside world until the 1870s. Yet Arizona — a hotbed of danger where Spanish, Mexican, Indian, and Anglo cultures mingled — beckoned with siren songs of silver and gold deposits, lost mines, buried treasure, and a surprisingly promising future.

Browne's Arizona adventure began unexpectedly the first Saturday in December, 1863. That day, in San Francisco, he encountered longtime friend Charles D. Poston, who, after lobbying Congress to recognize Arizona as a territory, became its first Superintendent of Indian Affairs. Now on his way to help organize the first territorial government, Poston invited Browne on an Arizona tour. Browne hurried home to Oakland, packed some clothes, sketching materials, and a meerschaum pipe into a knapsack, bid good-bye to his wife and eight children, and joined Poston aboard a southbound steamer.

Disembarking at San Pedro, Los Angeles' port, Poston's 10-man party joined its six-soldier escort at nearby Camp Drum. Besides Poston and Browne, the group included a freed slave as cook, a Pima chief, an Indian agent, a U.S. marshal, and a pair of Franciscan priests. After a 12-day journey by wagon, mule, and horseback, part of it across the Colorado Desert, the men arrived at Fort Yuma on Arizona's Colorado River border.

On the opposite bank stood Arizona City, the hamlet of 151 people known later as Yuma. Mesquite and cottonwood trees dotted the riverbank, willows grew above the Colorado-Gila junction, all amidst an "atmosphere of wonderful richness" bathed in "a gorgeous canopy of prismatic colors." Browne was impressed by Arizona City's December weather — "finer than that of Italy" — though he guessed summer's heat was so dry that "there is no juice left in anything living or dead," and chickens "come out of the shell ready cooked."

On December 31, Browne and his companions left Fort Yuma and began an eight-day, 120-mile journey along the Gila River to the Pima Villages east of the river's big bend. Although the Gila was nearly dry that time of year, its mesquite-clogged bottomlands teemed with flocks of water birds and coveys of quail.

The first night out Browne camped at deserted Gila City. Gold, discovered there in 1858, had built the boom town, but the boom went bust. "At the time of our visit," Browne reported, "the promising metropolis of Arizona consisted of three chimneys and a coyote."

The pace of travel was set by the distance between water holes. Sometimes Browne and his comrades made a leisurely 20 to 25 miles a day. If water was scarce they tried for twice that, starting out in the afternoon, stopping at midnight, setting out again at daylight, and halting around midday.

The danger of encountering Apaches was all too real — some men Browne met died in clashes with them only weeks later — so the travelers were understandably relieved when, after journeying along the Gila Trail, they reached the Pima Villages. These 10 Pima and two Maricopa settlements on both sides of the Gila River — among them Sacaton, Santan, and Snaketown — "have afforded the only protection ever given to American citizens in Arizona."

After a brief detour to the Casa Grande ruins, a four-day, 70-mile journey south led to a "scatteration of human habitations" populated by "traders, speculators, gamblers, horse-thieves, murderers, and vagrant politicians." In other words, Tucson, which Browne also described as "a city of mud-boxes, dingy and dilapidated, cracked and baked into a composite of dust and filth; littered about with broken canals, sheds, bakeovens, carcasses of dead animals, and broken pottery, barren of verdure, parched, naked, and grimly desolate in the glare of a southern sun." The best accommodations a visitor "can possibly expect are the dried mud walls of some unoccupied outhouse."

Browne's party stayed only long enough to requisition an escort of soldiers. Riding south past San Xavier del Bac mission ("one of the most beautiful and picturesque edifices to be found on the North American continent"), Browne entered the strikingly verdant valley of the Santa Cruz River with its thickets of mesquite, stands of cottonwoods, and "waving fields of grass, from two to four feet high."

Although the area abounded with bear, wild turkey, rabbits, antelope, and deer, its non-Apache population was virtually nil. Here the heat of the tribal blast proved particularly intense. "Wherever our attention was attracted by the beauty of the scenery or the richness of the soil, a stone-covered grave marked the foreground," Browne wrote.

"The ranches were in ruin; south and east of Tucson there was not a single inhabited spot within the boundary lines," Browne noted. The first night out he camped at Rhode's Ranch, a ruin. The following day he took lunch at Calabasas, also in ruin, near the remains of the Pennington Ranch. Here, "Old Pennington" had resisted waves of Apaches: "His cattle were stolen, his corrals burned down, his fields devastated; yet he bravely stood it out to the last." Finally, even Eli Pennington called it quits and moved out.

At the end of the second day's ride Browne reached Tubac, site of a Spanish presidio built in 1752 and, starting in 1856, nerve center of Charlie Poston's mining operations. Here the *Weekly Arizonian*, Arizona's first newspaper, began publication in 1859, but in 1861 Apaches forced Tubac's abandonment. "Tubac is now a city of ruins — ruin and desolation wherever the eye rests," Browne reported. Not a soul lived there in 1864. Tubac's gardens had "afforded a pleasant place of retreat in summer, with their shady groves of acacia and peach trees . . . ." But now Browne saw that "the old Plaza was knee deep with weeds and grass. All around were adobe houses, with the roofs fallen in and the walls crumbling to ruin."

Near present-day Nogales grass "up to our horses' shoulders covered the Valley" and "the hills were clothed with luxuriant groves of oak." After looping into Mexico and back into Arizona, the intrepid travelers arrived at Mowry Mine in the oak-covered Santa Rita Mountains near what is now Patagonia.

> Here we found the first indications we had enjoyed for some weeks of life and industry. Cords of wood lay piled up on the wayside; the sound of the axe reverberated from hill to hill;

the smoke of many charcoal pits filled the air, and teamsters, with heavily-laden wagons, were working their way over the rugged trails and by-paths . . . . Down in a beautiful little valley of several hundred acres, almost embosomed in trees, stand the reduction works, store-houses, and peon quarters of the Mowry Silver Mines.

Moving on, Browne returned to rest in Tubac a few days, taking notes and drawing, although sketching was tricky business with Apaches never far off. "I never before traveled through a country in which I was compelled to pursue the fine arts with a revolver strapped around my body, a double-barrelled shot-gun lying across my knees, and half a dozen soldiers armed with Sharpe's carbines keeping guard in the distance . . . . An artist with an arrow in his back may be a very picturesque object to contemplate at one's leisure; but I would rather draw him on paper than sit for the portrait myself."

On a week-long ride Browne and Poston inspected the abandoned mines to the west. On the way to the Santa Rita Mine, for example, he passed the grave of its former manager. "A marble head-stone, upon which his name is inscribed, with the additional words, not uncommon in Arizona, 'Killed by the Apaches,' marks the spot. By the side of his grave is another head-stone, bearing the name of Mr. Slack, his predecessor . . . . Another of the managers, also killed by the Apaches, lies buried at Tubac."

Returning to Tucson the last week of February, Browne and Poston engaged "the services of six Papago Indians, a Mexican, an American, and a jackass, with which formidable escort we took our departure from Tucson." At the Pima Villages, the two men parted company. Poston rode north to the town site which residents three months later voted to call Prescott. (That summer he was elected Arizona's first congressional delegate.) Browne found himself a place in the wagon of a merchant bound for Fort Yuma and was back home in Oakland by April.

Word of Browne's Arizona adventures preceded his arrival. Two "Ross Browne Letters" had already been published in a San Francisco newspaper and eight more appeared later. Soon *Harper's Monthly* picked up the series, transformed five years later into *A Tour Through Arizona, 1864, or Adventures in the Apache Country*, the first lengthy, well-received, widely popular account of Arizona. Beneath the mining statistics, the wit, and one-liners, Browne displayed an appreciation for Arizona. He described Arizona's natural beauty in superlative terms, praising the "unclouded sky and glowing tints of the mountains; the unbounded opulence of sunshine, which seemed to sparkle in atmosphere scintillations . . . . Such sunrises and sunsets, such marvelous richness of coloring, such magic lights and shades, I have never seen equalled in Europe, not even in Italy or the islands of the Grecian Archipelago."

After this journey, Browne continued to travel and wrote more books and articles. He revisited Arizona only once, though, a year later when, as a captain in the U.S. Army, he rode the Colorado River steamboat *Cocopah* from Fort Mojave to Yuma. But it had been enough. And when he died in Oakland in 1875, it could be said that John Ross Browne and his Arizona rambles focused national attention not only on Arizona's short-term dangers but also on its long-term potential as an economic and environmental bonanza.

Dr. George Emery Goodfellow

He loved the excitement of the boom towns of the West and was a devotee of their saloons and dance halls, but Dr. George Emery Goodfellow of Tombstone was also a well-respected physician known nationally for his pioneering work in the treatment of gunshot wounds.

B Y   L E O   W .   B A N K S

———◆◆◆———

G EORGE EMERY GOODFELLOW LIVED A LIFE AS BIG AS THE frontier. The two were made for each other, and much alike: hearty, impulsive, grand, full of appetites and the will to satisfy them.

He was a doctor during Tombstone's boom years and once said that a good surgeon needed "the eye of an eagle, the heart of a lion, and the touch of a woman."

Goodfellow had all three in abundance. He treated so many gut-shot miners and gamblers that he was known nationwide for his skill at plucking lead out of perforated abdomens. They called him the first civilian trauma surgeon.

He was born December 23, 1855, in Downieville, California. His father, Milton J. Goodfellow, came west in the gold rush and wound up practicing medicine and dentistry in the wide-open camps that sprang up amid the fever for metal.

No matter that Milton Goodfellow was an engineer who'd studied medicine in college but never graduated. He was the only one around to do the job. Everyone called him Doc.

Young George followed his father's lead, but only after his military career was derailed by prejudice. Goodfellow was a freshman at the University of California in 1871 when he declined an opportunity to attend West Point because the Army had recently admitted blacks.

In June of the following year, he won appointment to the U.S. Naval Academy, unaware that institution also was changing its white-only admission policy.

Navy records show that at Annapolis he joined with other midshipmen in a campaign of harassment against James Conyers, the academy's first black cadet.

On December 12, 1872, Goodfellow was expelled for using "profane and vulgar language, in a provoking and reproachful spirit and manner" toward Conyers, and for assaulting him.

In a letter to the secretary of the Navy seeking reinstatement, Goodfellow "denied all charges except that of pushing him (Conyers) on the stairs of the quarters . . . which I then, and now, seriously regret." His request was refused.

Some believe Goodfellow underwent a change in his racial attitudes after becoming a doctor. He was known to treat anybody who needed help, regardless of race or ability to pay.

After the Annapolis mess, Goodfellow graduated from Cleveland's Wooster University Medical School in 1876, married Katherine Colt, and moved to Oakland to begin private practice.

But ordinary life offered him none of the excitement he craved. At the suggestion of his father, he took a job in Prescott as company doctor at a mine. Then he worked briefly as a surgeon at Fort Whipple, and in 1879-1880, he was a contract surgeon at Fort Lowell in Tucson.

It was during this time that Tombstone was born, and the tales of abundant silver and 24-hour saloons presented the kind of howling life Goodfellow wanted. The doctor arrived in the boomtown in September, 1880.

He was 24, a popular, pugnacious, blue-eyed dandy. He had an office above the swank Crystal Palace Saloon and was a fixture at the Can Can, another drinking and gambling establishment.

When not buying rounds for the house or playing faro, he could usually be found trading whispers with one of the camp's finest prostitutes. Goodfellow was a married man and a rounder, a fact known to his daughter, Edith, who once remarked that her father was "always a gentleman in his love affairs."

But nothing could keep the dedicated doctor from his patients, many of whom were outlaws. Curly Bill Brocius and his boys shot each other up so often that Goodfellow practically made a living off them.

"Many a time a man would ride up to my house at night, get me out of bed and tell me one of the boys was hurt, that he was at Curly Bill's Camp," said Goodfellow in *Billy King's Tombstone*, by historian Carl Leland Sonnichsen.

"I would go with him and find several holes in his hide made hyperdermically with a gun that was loaded. I never asked how it happened . . . . My object was to see if I could save him. Also I was interested in my fee. I always got a good one."

As a doctor, he was bold. In January, 1889, a man named R.A. Clark was shot in the belly in Bisbee, and Goodfellow was summoned. He cut into his patient on a restaurant table, assisted by hard-handed miners and a barber who administered the anesthetic.

The *Tombstone Prospector* described the remarkable operation: "He opened his abdomen, took his intestines out and laid them on his chest . . . picked out the two bullets in the intestines . . . and replaced them (intestines), sewed up the skin, and the wounded man was conversing with the doctor a short time afterward."

Clark later died. But Goodfellow argued in a medical paper that the operation was justified because it "gave him about 18 hours of life, enabling him to make a will and to attend to such business affairs as were necessary."

In numerous other cases, Goodfellow's patients lived, disproving the commonly-held view that surgery was of little value in abdominal gunshot wounds.

Goodfellow also did cataract surgery and delivered babies. He even performed plastic surgery on a friend, accepting only a couple of bottles of whiskey and some cigars as payment.

The 1880s in Tombstone were violent years, and Goodfellow was in the thick of it. He helped coroner Harry Matthews perform autopsies on Billy Clanton and the McLaury brothers after their fight with the Earp brothers near the O.K. Corral.

Two months later, when Virgil Earp was shot-gunned from ambush, Goodfellow picked more than 20 pellets of lead shot from Virgil's body and removed four inches of bone from his left arm, probably saving it from amputation.

The doctor was also part of the mob that lynched

prisoner John Heith from a telegraph pole on Toughnut Street in February of 1884. Because Goodfellow was county coroner at the time, his presence, and probable participation, presented a small problem, which he got around in his final report. It stands as a classic in the West's literature of the macabre:

"He came to his death from emphysema of the lungs, which might've been, and probably was, caused by strangulation, self-inflicted or otherwise . . . . Emphysema was . . . sometimes due to the effects of high altitude (failure to keep your feet on the ground). All agreed that it was an uplifting ceremony."

Goodfellow was a civic leader, too, instrumental in building Tombstone's first swimming pool and helping develop a system for piping water into town, rather than hauling it in barrels. But his wide-ranging interests most often involved adventure.

He rode with the Army in pursuit of Geronimo in 1886, and in May of 1887, he stocked a wagon with medical supplies and hurried south to Bavispe, Sonora, Mexico to treat the victims of a devastating earthquake. His mercy mission earned him the lasting affection of Sonorans and the nickname El Santo Doctor.

Two years after being declared a saint, Goodfellow plunged a knife into a man named Frank White on a Tombstone street, leaving a serious, but not fatal, wound.

The *Epitaph* provided few details of the August, 1889, encounter: "There had been bad blood between the two men for some time, but for what reason is not known." The doctor was fined $25 for carrying a concealed weapon.

Goodfellow's 1891 departure from Tombstone was straight out of a dime novel. It happened when Dr. John C.

Handy, first Chancellor of the University of Arizona and surgeon for Southern Pacific Railroad, was shot on a Tucson street by his wife's divorce lawyer.

Telegraph wires to Tombstone sizzled with the wounded Handy's plea: "Get Goodfellow."

With daughter Edith at his side, the doctor hopped a train and drove it to Tucson himself, pushing the throttle to a speed that had the trainmen thinking this might be their last ride.

A.S. Reynolds, whose recollections are on file at the Arizona Historical Society in Tucson, was aboard the speeding train:

"I was very busy hanging onto the grab iron on the side of the caboose cupola to keep from being thrown out of my seat . . . . From there [Vail's Station] to Tucson the track is straight down hill. We sure was going some at that time. It was more like being shot out of a large gun than running on wheels."

Goodfellow wasn't able to save Handy, but he was offered the dead man's job as Southern Pacific surgeon, and took it.

In his five years in Tucson, Goodfellow continued to show remarkable energy and innovation — buying a hotel and converting it into a private hospital, performing Arizona Territory's first appendectomy, and probably the world's first prostate removal surgery.

Miley Wesson, writing in a medical magazine in 1933, reported that some eastern doctors, provincial in their belief that no medical breakthrough could occur in a God-forgotten desert town, doubted Goodfellow's claim and looked on him as an imposter.

The doctor's last great adventure came during the Spanish-American War when he volunteered to serve as a surgeon on the staff of an old friend, Maj. Gen. William Shafter. Not only was Goodfellow in on the invasion of Cuba, but he also helped negotiate the Spanish surrender at Santiago in July, 1898.

He wore a blindfold and made several dangerous trips behind enemy lines to meet with Gen. José Toral, the Spanish commander. Goodfellow used his fluent command of Spanish, rough charm, and whiskey to win over the general.

"Alcohol has never been used for a better or a more therapeutic cause," said Goodfellow.

But his last years were unhappy. In 1900 he moved to San Francisco and was living at the St. Francis Hotel six years later when the great earthquake struck. Everything he owned was gone, except his collection of Oriental rugs, which he'd loaned to singer Enrico Caruso for a performance.

Wesson wrote that the situation was made worse when two friends, investors with Goodfellow in a building leveled in the quake, withdrew from the deal leaving him to shoulder the financial loss.

Goodfellow was a bitter man when he departed California a year later to become chief surgeon for Southern Pacific in Guaymas, Mexico. That was also the year the last of his 13 medical papers was published. Writing in

Scientific American, Goodfellow declared the poisonous bite of a Gila monster was not fatal.

According to Wesson, his research consisted in part of teasing one of the reptiles until it bit him, then waiting to see if he'd die. Goodfellow concluded that fear of Gila monsters was a "remnant of primitive man's antagonism to all creeping things."

The doctor's last days were spent in excruciating pain and despair. He fell ill with multiple neuritis, a disease of the nerves that eventually left him unable to use his hands. He told his doctor, son-in-law C.W. Fish, that he'd rather die than live without being able to perform surgery.

With his condition worsening, Goodfellow departed Guaymas early in March, 1910, and died in a Los Angeles hospital nine months later. The man known as the gun-fighters' surgeon was only 54, but in that short time he lived enough for 10 men.

Zane Grey

Best-selling author Zane Grey loved Arizona,
often featuring the state as the setting for his
books and modeling his characters on Arizonans
he'd met during his lengthy stays there.
The love affair ended abruptly, however,
over hunting regulations, and the
outdoorsman-author never returned to the
state he had brought to a huge audience.

B Y   J O S E P H   S T O C K E R

IN THE SPRING OF 1907, AT FLAGSTAFF, ARIZONA TERRITORY, a man stepped off a train from the East. He was in his mid-30s, 5-feet 9-inches tall, slight of build, but giving off an aura of quiet strength. He had trim, even features and high cheek bones (there was a trace of Indian in him). His hair was black and plentiful and parted in the middle.

The man's name was Zane Grey. He had first visited Arizona the previous year and had become enamored then with what he perceived as a surviving remnant of the frontier, the true West, clean, magnificent, unspoiled. Now he was back to explore Arizona, study its people, write about them, and — although he couldn't know it at the time — have quite an impact on the state he came to love.

In due course, this Ohio-born dentist-turned-author would emerge as one of the most prodigious producers of the printed word in the history of American writing. Over a career that was to last another 30-odd years, he turned out 81 books. More than 130 million copies were sold. Hollywood made well over 100 movies from them. At least half his books used Arizona settings and/or Arizonans as characters, some of them based on the people he met. He visited Arizona 20 or more times, often spending weeks or months here.

Through the years Zane Grey also was to become a controversial figure in Arizona, provoking debate to this day.

The occasion for the 1907 trip was to hunt for mountain lions. Accompanying Grey was an aging but colorful character known as Buffalo Jones. In his earlier years Jones had mowed down buffalo by the dozens and now, stricken by conscience, was dedicated to helping the species survive. He had a buffalo ranch on the Rim of the Grand Canyon.

Grey, still in his fledgling years as an author and the possessor of a formidable collection of rejection slips, wrote a book about Jones called *The Last of the Plainsmen*. A publisher said: "I don't see anything in this to convince me that you can write either narrative or fiction."

Grey picked himself up off the floor, made another trip to Flagstaff and northern Arizona and produced his first two Western romances, *Heritage of the Desert* and *Riders of the Purple Sage*. Both sold. (Actually *Purple Sage* was rejected at first as too "bulgy" — Grey did tend to run off at the pencil with long descriptions and self-indulgent philosophizing. But the wife of a publisher's vice president stayed up until 3:00 one morning reading it and loved it.) And Zane Grey was on his way.

Purple Sage got him into his first Arizona ruckus,

though. The book was about Mormons, whom Grey liked, and polygamy, which he hated. He admired the Mormons' pioneering fortitude and their struggle to survive in the inhospitable environment of the Arizona Strip, that yawning, desolate land above the Grand Canyon. But he pitied the Mormon women — mistreated victims of plural marriage in his eyes. And his criticism went beyond polygamy to include what he saw as the fanaticism and greed of the frontier Mormon hierarchy. Quite a few Mormons took umbrage. "One woman here told me that her mother walked out the door when Zane Grey came, saying 'You're no good,'" recalls Marguerite Noble, Payson historian and author of her own Western novel, *Filaree.*

Grey came back to northern Arizona again to study the Navajos and Hopis. An Indian, Nasja Begay, led him on a strenuous expedition overland to Rainbow Bridge (they lacked the convenient accessibility of a boat ride on modern-day Lake Powell). It is widely accepted that Grey was only the third white man to see Rainbow Bridge, and he probably gave it its name. "Here," he wrote, entranced, "was rainbow magnified even beyond dreams, a thing not transparent and ethereal, but solidified, a work of ages, sweeping up majestically from the red walls, its iris-hued arch against the blue sky."

Grey wrote books about the Indians. He applauded what Candace C. Kant, in her book *Zane Grey's Arizona,* describes as "the Indians' struggle to retain their culture and, at the same time, accommodate newcomers to their land." But he thought the Indians were a dying race. The current population of the Navajo reservation alone — some 165,000 — suggests that Zane Grey may have been a bit premature.

He took a look at the Mexican border and southern Arizona and sited at least three of his Western romances in that desert region. One of the Mexican revolutions of the early 20th century was going on at the time. Grey filtered his stories through the resultant turmoil and revealed, in the process, a rather strong distaste for the Mexicans. He liked the "true Spanish," but he thought the Mexicans ruthless and cruel. He particularly faulted them for throwing out the Yaqui Indians. He "felt that racial mixture (i.e., Spanish with Indian) produced corruption and degeneration," says Candace Kant.

Grey settled in for a while at a cabin in Oak Creek Canyon and wrote *Call of the Canyon*. It had a familiar Zane Grey theme: The decadent, materialistic East versus the strong, pure, honest West, a place of gutsy, straight-shooting heroes and pure and wholesome heroines. Grey's dislike of the East may have been influenced somewhat by the brickbats flung at him by New York-based literary critics. They thought his themes simplistic, his stories two-dimensional, his dialogue stilted, his West idealized and romanticized. "It is difficult to imagine any writer having less merit in either style or substance than Grey and still maintain an audience at all," wrote Burton Rascoe in *The Saturday Review.*

Zane Grey, of course, wept all the way to the bank.

About the time of World War I he heard of the so-called Pleasant Valley War. It was a rancher-versus-rustler family feud taking place in the region of the Mogollon Rim, that great forested escarpment stretching 200 miles through middle-upper Arizona into New Mexico.

Grey hired a guide to take him into the Rim country to hunt bear and mountain lion and try to get at the facts of the Pleasant Valley War. In the process, he took a fancy to the region ("a split, tossed, dimpled, heaving, rolling world of black-green forestland"). He bought three of those black-green acres from a homesteader named A.L. "Babe" Haught and had a cabin built below the Rim.

There, during the 1920s, Zane Grey sat in a Morris chair, writing on a board across his lap, and producing some of his most popular books. (One of his secretaries said later that he made notes for the books at the Rim cabin but did the actual writing at his homes in Pennsylvania and California.)

The Rim output totaled — it is said — 14 books in all. They included a pair of his best-sellers, *To the Last Man*, his story of the Pleasant Valley War, and *Under the Tonto Rim*. (Grey simply renamed the Mogollon Rim, reasoning, apparently, that nobody could pronounce "Mogollon." He borrowed Tonto from the Tonto Apaches. As you'd see if you visited nearby Payson, the name has stuck. A lot of things around there are called Tonto.)

Grey had a way of putting the people he met into his books. Jim Emett, a Mormon patriarch who, for a while, ran Lees Ferry on the Colorado River, inspired the character of the Mormon patriarch August Nash in *Heritage of the Desert*. Emett's son, Snap, didn't like Grey when he met him, made it clear that he didn't, and turned up vengefully in the book as Snap Naab, a mean man who beat his wife. John and Louisa Wetherill, who ran a trading post at Kayenta, appeared in the *The Vanishing American* as a couple named Withers, operating a trading post at a fictional place called Kaibab.

Now, working in the Rim country, Grey did the same with the Haught family. Babe's son, Edd, became Edd Denmeade in *Under the Tonto Rim*. His sister, Myrtle, became Mertie Denmeade. "He put all of us in some book or other," said Myrtle.

Many things around Payson are named for Zane Grey. The whole Rim region is often called Zane Grey Country. And there are the Zane Grey Twirlers, a square dance group; the Kiwanis Club of Zane Grey Country; the American Heart Association, Zane Grey Division. There's even a national organization of Zane Grey fans, Zane Grey's West Society, headed by a veterinarian living in Maryland. Members call themselves Zanies.

But not everybody worships the ground Zane Grey walked on. For one thing, fairly or not, he gained the reputation as a womanizer. Although he was married, he left his wife at home while numbers of secretaries accompanied him on his hunting trips, and it was bruited about that they didn't spend all their time taking dictation. The *New Times*, a Phoenix weekly newspaper, in an article in November, 1987, bluntly called them "concubines of the month." Candace Kant implicitly confirms the gossip. There was "a sensual side to Grey," she writes, "apparent in his love of beautiful women."

Not long ago, when the Payson school board voted not to name a new school Zane Grey Elementary, replacing Payson Elementary, it was widely supposed that Grey's alleged womanizing figured in the decision. Marianne Morrison, a board member, claims it had more to do with economics. The school system had a lot of letterheads and things left over with the imprint of Payson Elementary School and didn't want to waste them.

The noisiest Zane Grey controversy of all attended his leave-taking of Arizona. (It may have figured as well in the school-naming episode.) Grey asked the state game commission for permission to shoot bear out of season. It was refused. Grey announced he was leaving Arizona and would never return, and he didn't.

As with most arguments, there were two sides to this one. A film crew was coming into the state to shoot the bear-killing. A good deal of money was tied up in the undertaking — money that would benefit the state's economy. Unbeknownst to Grey, the bear season had been changed. Grey thought that, considering all the publicity he'd given Arizona and all the money that movie studios spent here filming his books, he deserved special consideration. The state disagreed.

In 1939, at the age of 64, Zane Grey died. His cabin, unattended, beset by vandals, fell into near ruin. Then, in the 1960s, William H. Goettl, a Phoenix air-conditioning manufacturer and Zane Grey fan, bought the Grey property and rebuilt the cabin. With the help of the author's heirs, he filled it with Grey artifacts — a Morris chair with writing boards, quantities of Zane Grey books, a hunting rifle, animal heads, and, ironically, a bear skin. The cabin became a major Payson sightseeing attraction. Mel Counseller, latest of a succession of curators, says as many as 20,000 people a year from all over the world visited the cabin.

In 1990, in what was called the Dude fire, after Dude Creek where lightning ignited the 28,000-acre conflagration, the Grey cabin was destroyed.

Today there is little to be seen at the cabin site — a few remnants of the cabin's rock foundation, an overgrowth of weeds, a well, once dry, now producing water because the trees now burned and dead, no longer drink it underground. High above, just beneath the Rim itself, spread many acres of blackened poles that had been green ponderosa pines.

A few of the cabin's artifacts were spared — a hunting rifle, clothing, some first edition Zane Grey books, his hat, chaps, a jacket. They can be seen today in Payson's Museum of the Forest. Those things — and the image of a wild and wonderful Arizona for millions of readers worldwide — are what Zane Grey, the super-author of tales of a West that may never have been, has bequeathed to the Arizona he once loved.

CHAPTER SEVEN

Jacob Hamblin

*Mormon missionary to the Indians
and wilderness explorer in the rugged,
empty Colorado Plateau, Jacob Hamblin
negotiated treaties with the Navajos and Utes,
opening the region to white settlers.*

BY LARRY WINTER

———⋙◆⋘———

A DISEMBODIED VOICE SPOKE TO JACOB HAMBLIN IN THE wilderness. "If you do not seek Indian blood," the voice promised, "No Indian will ever take yours." The promise was timely, for just then Hamblin was locked in mortal combat with a Ute warrior. Although both men had been out on the same errand that winter day in 1851 — rounding up range cattle that had strayed from remote Mormon ranches — their goals conflicted: Hamblin aimed to return the cattle to the ranchers; the Ute wanted to collect them for a new set of owners, his fellow tribesmen.

What began as a pitched battle degenerated into a rock fight after Hamblin's gun jammed and the Ute ran out of arrows. Yet the fight proved no less deadly once the men reverted to more primitive weapons. When the voice spoke, Hamblin was hoisting a heavy boulder into the air while the exhausted Ute lay panting at his feet. They had fought all afternoon, and Hamblin meant to finish the fight once and for all by crushing the Ute's skull. Only the voice, soft yet authoritative, stopped him. Dumbstruck,

Hamblin let the boulder fall to his feet while the Ute, oblivious to spirit voices but intent on survival, vanished into a nearby thicket.

A few years later Hamblin was called again. This time, however, the voice was not that of an incorporeal spirit, but of the Mormon leader, Brigham Young. "Feed Indians, rather than fight them," Young commanded when he appointed Hamblin to lead the Mormon's Southern Indian Mission in 1855. Following Young's instructions, Hamblin extended a helping hand to every wanderer — Indian or Anglo — he met during the next 30 years as he explored, often alone, the empty quarters of southern Utah and northern Arizona.

A committed polygamist, Hamblin took five wives, including one Paiute, during his long life. His mission led him and his families from central to southern Utah, then to the Arizona Strip, and finally across the Colorado River to the White Mountains of Arizona. Like other devout Mormons of his time, he believed Indians were the remnants of the Lamanites, one of the last of the lost tribes of Israel. To return them to the circle of the elect he had to learn their languages and ways.

"I was born a white man," Hamblin once observed, "I've always wanted to be a white man. But somehow, in the shuffle of life, the Lord made me over into an Indian."

Shortly before he heard the voice in the wilderness, Hamblin led a party of Mormon settlers after another band of Ute rustlers. When they surprised the Indians at daybreak, the Utes sought to avoid a fight. A few scrawny cows hardly seemed worth killing over. The Ute chief approached Hamblin under a flag of truce before the fight could start in earnest. "If you shoot, I must. But if you do not, I need not," the chief pointed out with impeccable logic. Hamblin accepted the truce, especially when the Utes offered to return the cattle. A fight surely would have entailed losses on both sides.

As part of the bargain, Hamblin demanded the Utes return with him to the Mormon settlement of Tooele where he hoped to negotiate a permanent end to cattle thieving. But the settlers at Tooele, fed up with rustling, had other ideas. Matters came to a head when the Mormons formed a firing squad to execute the Utes. Heedless of the consequences, Hamblin jumped in front of the Ute chief and dared the squad. "Go on, shoot," he cried, "Only let me be first." The settlers reluctantly spared the Indians.

Then two legends began to grow, one, among whites, of Jacob, the Indian-lover, who might even be a traitor to his kind; the other, among Indians, of the white man who would die for his word. Whites, who often resented Hamblin's scrupulous fairness to Indians, nonetheless relied upon him to blaze their trails and make the peace needed to expand their settlements. They called him the "Leatherstocking of the West" in grudging acknowledgment. Paiutes, Hopis, even the fearsome Navajos and Utes, called him "Father."

Hamblin once sent his son Jacob Jr. to trade a horse to Chuar'ruumpeak, a Paiute chief. Chuar'ruumpeak let the boy name his price for the horse. Sensing an opportunity to make a killing, young Jacob asked for double the real value of the horse. Chuar'ruumpeak agreed without argument, and the boy rode home thoroughly satisfied with his bargain. But when Jacob Sr. saw how unfair the trade had been, he made his son return half his loot. Chuar'ruumpeak began to laugh as soon as young

Jacob rode in sight. "I knew your father would not cheat me," the Paiute chuckled. "He is my father, too."

If any tribe appeared to be pure representatives of the Lamanites, it was the Hopis who were known to live in walled communities and practice a complex religion in church-like kivas. Between 1858 and 1873, Hamblin crossed the Colorado River six times to visit the Hopis.

On Hamblin's first mission to the Hopis, Brigham Young assigned him to investigate a competing theory of the origin of the Hopis: that they were really displaced Welshmen. Once the myth of a tribe of lost Welshmen was almost as prevalent in the West as the myth of Indian Israelites. Even Thomas Jefferson had believed it. Luckily for theology, James Davis, a bona fide Welshman brought along expressly for the purpose, could detect no trace of Welsh in the Hopis' language.

Hamblin learned the Hopis had legendary tribes of their own, including a tribe of mysterious white men who would eventually lead the Hopis across the Colorado, a journey that was otherwise taboo. However, the Hopis were not convinced Hamblin's was the expected party, so he could not induce any of them to return with him to the Mormon settlements.

Crossing the Colorado Plateau in those days called for epic endurance. The trail led through thick pine forests and across vast deserts. Navajos barred the way to Hopi-land with war parties. The most daunting obstacles, the inaccessible canyons of the great, red Colorado River cut the southern Colorado Plateau off from the north. Only a few fords, hidden in the deepest canyons, provided safe passage, and Hamblin explored nearly every one. Besides fording the Colorado at the Crossing of the Fathers for the first time since Escalante pioneered it in 1776, Hamblin also discovered Ute Crossing, Pearce Ferry, and Lees Ferry. He found Havasu Canyon, the previously unknown home of the Havasupai, while searching out new routes to Hopiland, but kept the pristine canyon's location secret, so great was his admiration for the idyllic life of the Havasupai.

In the fall of 1859, Young directed Hamblin to lead a yearlong mission to the Hopis, but the mission failed when a Navajo war party intercepted the Mormons and killed one of the missionaries, George A. Smith, the son of a Mormon Apostle. Three years later, Hamblin returned to Hopiland with a force of 20 men. "This time," Brigham Young told Hamblin, "keep your guns as handy as your Bibles." Fortunately, the Navajos were nowhere in sight, so Hamblin was not forced to test the promise made long before by the voice. This time the meeting with the Hopis went so well that he left three missionaries behind.

Another busy year for Hamblin was 1870. After finally persuading a few Hopis to visit the Mormon settlements beyond the Colorado River, he guided John Wesley Powell, then on his second expedition down the river, across the Colorado Plateau to Hopiland and on to Fort Defiance. There Hamblin and Powell negotiated a new peace with the Navajos who were still raiding Mormon settlements in southern Utah despite the peace treaty they had signed in 1868 with the federal government.

Hamblin played a crucial role in the new negotiations. Later Powell wrote of him, "He is a silent, reserved man, and when he speaks it is in a slow, quiet way that inspires great awe." Indeed, one of Hamblin's short speeches carried the day. "I now have gray hairs on my head," he told the assembled Navajo dignitaries, "And from boyhood I have been on the frontiers, doing all I could to preserve peace between white men and Indians. I despise this killing, this shedding of blood. I hope you will stop [raiding], and instead come visit and trade with our people."

On November 5, Barboncito and his fellow war chiefs agreed to a compact banning Navajo raiding while opening Mormon settlements to Navajo trade. This treaty, the crowning achievement of Hamblin's life, breached the last barrier to Mormon migration into the fertile White Mountains of Arizona. At Brigham Young's direction, Hamblin led a half dozen parties of Mormon settlers across Navajo land in the next decade.

But the peace was not an easy one to keep. In 1873, only three years after he had helped Powell negotiate with the Navajos, a party of miners killed three sons of a Navajo chief named Ketchenee and badly wounded a fourth. The Navajos mistakenly blamed the Mormons. Wearily Hamblin set off alone to stop another war, but at Mowabi he was joined by two non-Mormon brothers named Smith. From Mowabi the three rode to the camp of Mush-ah, a Navajo who had been friendly to Hamblin in the past. There Ketchenee, accompanied by a dozen or so young Navajos, found them and put Hamblin on trial as a surrogate for all Mormons.

Before entering the hogan, Hamblin strapped on a revolver one of his sons had made him bring. The Navajo warriors, who knew of the voice that had spoken to Hamblin many years before, recognized the significance of the gun. Once in the hogan, Hamblin patiently explained that miners, not Mormons, had attacked Ketchenee's sons, but the Navajos were not satisfied. After a lengthy argument, they announced the Smiths could leave, but Hamblin must die. The Smiths, however, declared that if one of the party were to get out alive, they all would.

As the Navajos growled and the Smiths reached for their guns, Hamblin had an inspiration. Taking his gun from its holster, he pondered it as if an unknown artifact had just fallen into his hand. The hogan fell silent. "This gun is in my way," Hamblin said after finally looking up. "What shall I do with it?" When no one answered, he tossed the revolver into the middle of the hogan. The Smiths hesitated, but then followed suit.

Hamblin started to explain again about the miners. Frustrated by Hamblin's deliberate vulnerability, not to mention his quiet persistence, a Navajo shouted, "Aren't you afraid?"

"Why should we be afraid of our friends?" Hamblin replied mildly. "Are not the Navajo our friends? Are we not theirs? Else why did we place ourselves in your power?"

The Navajo fell silent, then whispered animatedly among themselves. Their debate carried on for more than an hour. Finally Ketchenee offered to take 150 head of cattle as compensation, but Hamblin stubbornly refused. To accept was to admit Mormon guilt. This principled obstinacy was too much. Now the insolent white man must surely die.

"Are you not afraid?" the same Navajo brave shouted again. Every eye in the smoky hogan fixed on Hamblin. Stroking his jaw, he considered the question anew. At first he stared at the ground, then at the patch of sky visible through the hogan's smoke hole. He cocked his head to listen to the rush of the wind outside. Finally he searched the faces of his accusers.

"No," Jacob Hamblin answered at last, his quiet voice a whisper on the wind, "My heart has never known fear."

Ironically Hamblin had no sooner attained peace with his Indian neighbors, than the federal government declared war on him when it began enforcing statutes against polygamy in the 1880s. Hamblin, who still had two wives, refused to give up either. Driven into exile in Mexico, he returned to Arizona in 1886. By then 77 and worn out with fever, he soon died. His gravestone in the White Mountain hamlet of Alpine, reads simply, "Peacemaker in the Camp of the Lamanites."

John Hance

*An early trail builder, guide, and tourism
promoter at the Grand Canyon, John Hance
was also an exceptional raconteur. His tall
tales about the Canyon, the surrounding country,
and the people who visited the national park
are still told today.*

BY LARRY WINTER

———⟫•⟪———

JOHN HANCE PRACTICALLY INVENTED TOURISM AT THE GRAND
Canyon just before the turn of the last century when he
began leading parties of visitors from the South Rim to
the Colorado River. He built his new trail, which carries his
name, and the old trail before it, to smooth the way for his
clients. And it was his business, not to mention his plea-
sure, to foster their senses of wonder and humor during
the long trek down and back.

During his lifetime, Hance was celebrated throughout
the country for the yarns he spun while descending into the
Canyon. "To see the Canyon only," observed a noted traveler, Chester P. Dorland, "and not see Captain John Hance, is
to miss half the show." For $12 a day, a client got a horse,
a trip to the river, and Hance's expert services as a guide.
Tall tales, country wisdom, and corny jokes were free. "He
laughs with the giddy, yarns to the gullible, talks sense to
the sedate," Dorland went on to say, "and is a most excellent judge of scenery, human nature and life."

When pressed, Hance admitted he was called "Captain" because he had once led a gang of Texas horse thieves on a series of raids into Mexico. He went on to tell them the gang enjoyed considerable initial success but eventually grew careless and rode into an ambush in 1881. All night and part of the next day, a troop of *vaqueros* chased Hance and his men across the barren plains of western Chihuahua.

Eventually the gang scattered, but the relentless vaqueros stuck to Hance's trail. The chase was desperate, Hance swore to his audiences, and they were inclined to believe him, for Hance — bearded, dressed in a shabby but elegant brown velveteen suit, his eyes shaded by a wide sombrero — still looked the part of a bandit chief.

Frantic to shake pursuit, he charged into the middle of a vast buffalo herd and in the dust and confusion, jumped on the lead bull to disguise his tracks. This proved a tactical triumph, but a strategic error, for once started, the bull would not stop. At the head of his herd, the startled animal charged west, then north. Much as he wanted, Hance could not jump off for fear of being trampled in the stampede.

By the end of the third day the vaqueros, choked by dust and unable to penetrate the stampede, gave up the chase, leaving Hance to the tender mercies of the panicked herd. Nothing slowed their flight across the Southwest until early one morning Hance was jerked awake by the herd skidding to an abrupt halt. Taken unawares, Hance flew off the lead bull. While airborne he had just enough time to wonder what could have stalled the hot charge of that many buffalo. Hance got his answer when he landed and found himself hanging over the rim of the Grand Canyon.

In the 1890s, Hance maintained a tourists' camp on the South Rim near Grandview Point. His clients came in all stripes — lawyers, soldiers, students, professors, dilettantes, doctors, and dowagers — men and women with the leisure and grit to tour a West that was still a little wild. Only a few years earlier, the Canyon had been the sole domain of Indians, prospectors, and desperadoes; and its romantic past remained part of its attraction. Hance, of course, was prepared to fill in details of the old days even if he had to manufacture the facts.

One of Hance's clients had been a literal tenderfoot. Hance liked to tell the story of a visitor fresh off the Flagstaff stage who bounded into camp one evening. The stranger walked with an obvious spring in his step, although (he confided to anyone who showed the least interest) he could barely hobble across a room only a month before. Then he was a prisoner of his feet; now he could outleap a deer. The secret lay in his shoes, a custom pair of walking boots, their soles molded from an exotic compound of rubber scientifically designed to cushion weak feet.

Shortly after the man arrived, one of Hance's guides led him to a nearby embayment of the South Rim. There the unthinkable occurred: The dude, hopping down the trail like a rabbit on springs, bounced over the edge. In the blink of an eye, he went from admiring the setting sun to hurtling toward the Tonto Plateau 3,000 feet below. The shaken guide dashed back to camp where he roused Hance and the rest of his crew. With heavy hearts they gathered at the rim to scan the distant plateau for evidence of the dude's remains.

Imagine their surprise when the dude, far from lying

broken on the stony ground below, came flying out of the Canyon instead. He bounced even with the rim, but about 30 feet out, hung in midair for a moment, then fell into the void again. Down on the plateau he landed on his feet, but before he could stop, the tremendous spring in his soles shot him back to the rim.

While their client bounced in and out of the Canyon behind them, Hance and his crew puzzled over how to effect a rescue. Unfortunately the problem proved complex, and night fell before they could agree on a plan. In utter darkness they retired to camp, where the distant cries of the jumping man haunted their sleep. He had not eaten since the day before in Flagstaff, and now, after a long stagecoach ride and an evening of strenuous bouncing, the stranger moaned in an agony of hunger. He was lucky in just one thing, his feet didn't hurt.

Breakfast was bleak. The smell of frying bacon, carried over to the Canyon by light airs, increased the frequency of the man's cries. The wranglers reluctantly concluded only a quick and merciful death could end his misery. Fortunately, inspiration seized Hance just as his men pulled their guns and drew a bead on the bouncing stranger.

Commanding them to hold fire, he grabbed a lariat and ran to the rim where he lassoed the dude at the apex of his jump with a perfectly timed throw. The rope jerked tight, pulling the man right out of his shoes, which tumbled back into the abyss. Meanwhile Hance and his wranglers easily hauled the starving man over to the rim.

In the end, they had to shoot the shoes. Otherwise they'd still be bouncing in a remote bay of the Canyon, about 30 feet off the rim.

"God made the Canyon," wrote Buckey O'Neill, leader of the Rough Riders, "John Hance the trails. Without the other, neither would be complete." That's still true. Even today, Hance's name is written all over the Canyon: the New Hance Trail leads to Hance Rapids. A few miles down river is Hance Canyon which contains traces of the Old Hance Trail. Hance also prospected the Last Chance Mine on Horseshoe Mesa and worked an asbestos mine in Asbestos Canyon before he discovered tourists were easier to work than the ground.

And work them he did, often using their comments as fuel for his tall tales. Once a young botanist gushed, "You know, Captain Hance, the tree is a wonderful organism — it breathes." Hance thought a moment. "That explains something that's puzzled me a long time," he said at last. "I used to camp under a big mesquite tree, and night after night I was awakened by snoring. At first I blamed my horse; later I thought it must have been echoes of myself; but now I see it was that tree kept me awake with its snoring."

When a storm would fill the Canyon with clouds and tourists would lament that they obscured the view, Hance would claim it made getting around a lot easier. He told them he simply strapped on his snowshoes and waded to his destination across the tops of clouds soft as fleece.

Hance lived the last 20 years of his life at the Grand Canyon's El Tovar Hotel where he was an honored guest and storyteller. And he made no excuses about how he made his living. He once asked his friend Elizabeth Heiser, a pioneer rancher, " If I don't tell stories to them people, who will?"

He died in 1918 at age 80, proclaiming, "I have lived on expectations and mountain scenery." What a rich life it must have been.

Ira Hayes

*A quiet Pima Indian boy from the reservation
south of Phoenix joined the Marines in World
War II. His bravery in battle and a chance
photograph by a war correspondent catapulted
him to fame, a fame that he felt was unjustified
and that ultimately destroyed him.*

BY AL HEMINGWAY

———◆———

THE GOVERNMENT GAVE THE BRAVE MARINE A HERO'S
burial at Arlington National Cemetery. As a light
snow dusted the surrounding headstones, the
Marine color guard and his family laid his body to rest in
Section 34, Plot 479A. The gray Virginia landscape and the
cold, silent snow were ironic and foreign to this hero. He
was a Pima Indian from the hot desert of central Arizona
and had earned national fame during World War II fighting
in the steaming tropics of the South Pacific. But then, life,
ultimately, was ironic for Ira Hamilton Hayes.

He was a quiet, shy, sensitive human being who
was thrust into the limelight by the famous photograph
by Associated Press photographer Joe Rosenthal of the
Marines raising the American flag during the Battle for
Iwo Jima in February, 1945. The fame the picture brought,
Hayes never wanted and could never escape.

The media characterized Ira Hayes as a loner; a man
who could never belong. His image received the Hollywood

treatment in 1961 when Tony Curtis portrayed him in the movie entitled *The Outsider*. The film focused on his latter years and his repeated bouts with alcoholism, a disease he suffered only after becoming what he considered undeservedly famous.

These impressions, however, are only partially right. True, the unwanted fame that resulted from the photo did contribute to Hayes' inability to cope after the war, but he was not an "outsider" as the motion picture suggests. The young Pima's time in the United States Marine Corps, with the exception of his childhood, was the happiest of his short, troubled life.

Ira Hayes enlisted in the U.S. Marine Corps on August 26, 1942. The young, impressionable Pima underwent the harassment that all recruits, or "boots," receive at the hand of their tormentors, the drill instructors. He was given the sobriquet of "Chief," for obvious reasons.

Upon completion of recruit training, Hayes volunteered for paratrooper school. Before being accepted into this elite arm of the Marine Corps, he had to pass the grueling six-week course at Camp Gillespie, California. William Faulkner, a friend of Hayes, recalled: "The first time Ira and I jumped, he went from brown to white and I went from white to green. He hit the ground hard, like a sack of wet cement. We were both scared, but we did it."

Soon, jumping became old hat. Faulkner remembered: "On this particular jump, Ira was about two or three behind me in the plane. When my turn came I went out and my 'chute opened and I started to drop. Suddenly, something hit the top of my 'chute — it was Ira! He rolled off — in mid-air — laughing and carrying on as he went by me!"

On November 30, 1942, Ira Hayes was awarded the

coveted wings of a United States Marine paratrooper. It would remain one of the proudest moments of his life. Former paratrooper Jack Charles recalls Ira saying with pride: "I'm the only Pima Indian to become a Marine paratrooper."

Immediately following school, Hayes was transferred to Company K, 3rd Parachute Battalion. As their training continued, Hayes and his fellow "ParaMarines" established close ties. He felt a strong camaraderie with his new friends and wrote to his mother about the "swell guys" he was fortunate to serve with. They attained a sense of loyalty that was exceptional. Soon, however, this loyalty would be put to the ultimate test — combat — as the paratroopers departed for the Pacific.

United States forces invaded Bougainville, largest island in the Northern Solomons, on November 1, 1943. On December 3, the ParaMarines landed to relieve some of the weary units that had been fighting there since the beginning of the invasion. The Marines patrolled aggressively to locate and estimate the size of the Japanese army in the area.

Two squads from Company K were dispatched on December 7 to reconnoiter a small "spur" near Hill 1000, the regimental command post. Hayes was among them. Ed Castle, a close companion of Hayes, relates the patrol's harrowing events: "We were on the go all day . . . . It was getting dark and the patrol leader sent Ira Hayes and a couple of other Marines ahead to scout . . . they . . . estimated they saw a company of Japs . . . washing and bathing in the river . . . totally unaware of our presence."

The men dug in and kept silent. Castle continues: " . . . these Japs were cutting in fire lanes on our position

[Hill 1000] . . . you could reach out and grab their ankles, they were so close!"

The following morning, the Marines gathered their gear and silently slipped away. Castle remembers: "And we took off and we were on the run. No sooner did we get off there . . . that whole hill was bombed."

After escaping death on that patrol, Hayes' unit was ordered to seize the "spur" from the enemy. All day the ParaMarines assaulted the Japanese fortifications but were unable to drive them from the hill. Seventeen men from Hayes' platoon were killed. The next day the survivors of the battle retrieved the bodies of their fallen comrades. The horrible sight awaiting them would remain with the young Pima forever. Bill Faulkner remembers: "When we reached the spot . . . we found the Japs had . . . driven wooden stakes through their arms, chest, and legs, pinning them to the ground. One of the Marines who came with us to get the bodies had a brother who was one of the dead. It's tough seeing your brother like that."

On January 15, 1944, the 3rd Parachute Battalion departed Bougainville for the United States, and Ira Hayes was granted a 30-day leave. As he stepped off the bus in Phoenix, he had an emotional reunion with his family. To Nancy Hayes, her son appeared "older," different. Having witnessed the deaths of so many of his fellow paratroopers, he had undergone a metamorphosis. The first virtue a young man sheds in combat is his innocence, and the Indian youth had lost his in the "Green Hell" of Bougainville.

The Marine Corps disbanded the parachute battalions and reassigned the men into various battalions to form the 5th Marine Division. Reporting to Camp Pendleton,

California, after his leave, Ira Hayes was transferred to Company E, or Easy Company, 2nd Battalion, 28th Marines as a regular infantryman. Keith Rasmussen, a former paratrooper, shared a tent with Hayes: "Although not expansive in social contact, Hayes was not the 'loner' as portrayed by later chroniclers. He carried himself with a self-confidence that immediately earned his comrades' respect. There was never any doubt in my mind that he belonged."

After months of intense training, the Leathernecks set sail for the island of Iwo Jima, landing there on February 19, 1945. The next four days Hayes was involved in some of the worst combat of the war in the Pacific. The 28th Marines literally inched their way toward Mount Suribachi, a 554-foot inactive volcano transformed into an impregnable fortress by the Japanese. Since Suribachi was the highest point on Iwo Jima, it had to be captured immediately.

At 8:00 A.M. on February 23, a 40-man combat patrol was formed from Easy Company's 3rd Platoon to scale the northeast slope of Suribachi. Two hours later, after the Marines had reached the crest of Suribachi, a small flag, measuring 54 by 28 inches, was hoisted. The island erupted with fog horns, bells, and whistles to signal that the volcano was now in American hands.

Lt. Col. Chandler Johnson, 2nd Battalion commander, wanted the flag as a souvenir. Besides he thought the flag was too small to see anyway. The decision was made to put up a larger flag. One was procured from a ship offshore and given to the battalion runner, Pfc. Rene Gagnon. On his way to the top, he joined Pfc. Ira Hayes, Sgt. Mike Strank, Pfc. Franklin Sousley, and Cpl. Harlon Block, who were laying communication wire.

When the party climbed to the summit, the bigger

flag was fastened to a piece of drainage pipe. As Hayes, Sousley, Block, Strank, Gagnon, and Navy Corpsman John Bradley struggled to lift it, Associated Press photographer Joe Rosenthal snapped the picture. The rest is history.

Unfortunately, Rosenthal did not develop his own pictures. After numbering them aboard a ship offshore, they were flown to Guam. When the picture of Hayes and the others was developed, it created an immediate uproar. When he reached Guam, Rosenthal was beset by reporters asking if he had staged it. Thinking they meant another photo of a group shot he had taken afterward, he said yes. However, when he saw the now-famous picture, he tried to explain that it was spontaneous, not posed. He never even knew the names of the six men in his picture until weeks later.

When the identity of the individuals was finally uncovered, Hayes, Gagnon, and Bradley were selected to return to the United States to participate in a War Bond drive. Sousley, Strank, and Block, had been killed during the fighting on Iwo Jima.

Hayes felt extremely guilty about his instant celebrity status. He felt he had done nothing heroic, yet, they were calling him a hero. He loathed the word. The real heroes to him were buried in the 5th Marine Division cemetery on Iwo Jima. To escape, he turned to alcohol. The bond tour only lasted two weeks for him. His repeated drinking was noticed by all, and he was ordered back to Easy Company. Keyes Beech, a Marine Corps combat correspondent, who accompanied Hayes on the bond tour, said years later: ". . . [it was] an agonizing experience for him, he was extremely shy. The only things that ever mattered to him was his mother and the Marine Corps."

In June, 1945, Hayes wrote to his relatives: "I am back again as you probably know, and I like it better this way. I have a reason for coming back. I hope you folks understand. Lots of guys don't. But I do. I do alone. And I swear I did the right thing. I've got my God to look up to and He has never failed me. It is by his protection that I did not stop a slug on Iwo. I felt his nearness many times. If it be God's will that I be unfortunate in a future battle, I will not be afraid, deep inside me, I will be prepared. There were a few guys who went all through the battle of Iwo with me. [We] fought together, and were scared most of the time together. And they were back here while I was in the States, just for raising a flag, and getting all the publicity and glory. That I could not see. These same guys may go into battle again and I would be with them. That is the way I feel about the whole affair. I feel well here among my buddy Marines, and once more feel like my old self. But there are too many of the old faces not around, and that is hard to forget . . . ."

Ira Hayes was honorably discharged on December 1,

1945. In retrospect, if Hayes had remained in the Marine Corps, it might have saved his life. It was his comfort zone. The Marine Corps would have been an insulator from the reporters and hero worshipers that hounded him until his dying day. Leo Bridal, a close friend, explains: "Ira seemed hesitant about leaving the Marine Corps and the fellowship that he had enjoyed during his stay . . . ."

The story of Ira Hayes' life has been told and retold in numerous newspaper and magazine articles, and in a short book, *The Hero of Iwo Jima* by William Bradford Huie. Every one of them concentrates on his later years, when his alcoholism progressively worsened. Each almost ignores perhaps the happiest period of his adult life — his tenure as a United States Marine. And that is the way Ira Hayes should be remembered.

According to Keith Rasmussen: "Ira was different, thereby making him so special in my memory. Is it because of the empathy that has grown over the intervening years for a man that did not wish to be singled out, because of the fluke of being in a certain place at a certain time, that would forever alter his life? Was he to pay penance for the last decade of his troubled life for having survived his ordeal? He would most assuredly have traded places with any of the three that were buried in the company of their buddies in the 5th Marine Division cemetery on that bleak island. His epitaph should simply have read: Ira Hayes . . . Marine! He would've liked that."

Pete Kitchen

*Legendary frontier rancher in the borderlands
south of Tucson, Pete Kitchen built his
fortress-ranch house along a well-worn Apache
raiding route. For decades he successfully
defended his family and employees
from Apaches and Mexican bandidos.*

B Y   R O N   M C C O Y

O N AUGUST 5, 1895, TUCSONANS NOTED WITH SADNESS the death of 73-year-old Pete Kitchen, a man whose life personified Arizona's frontier experience. Small wonder many folks who lived through those frenzied times felt strongly that word of Pete Kitchen's saga should be passed down. They never forgot the bloody days of the late 1860s and 1870s when, somehow, his ranch alone escaped Apache destruction in the corridor of lawlessness running between Tucson and the Mexican border.

Daily, Pete faced the sort of dangers that provided grist for the mills of popular fiction. "What these dangers were," the *Tucson Citizen* opined in Kitchen's obituary, "few people not actual participants in them can conceive or appreciate, but they were with him waking and sleeping." Some of Kitchen's friends swore that when asked how he managed to survive, Pete explained, "My motto was, 'If it ain't wearin' a hat, shoot it!'"

Contemporaries remembered Pete Kitchen as a rough-hewn character, a blue-eyed, red-faced, husky veteran of the pioneer era who liked games of chance, took a few drinks, and swore mightily. But beneath the grizzled exterior lay the softer stuff of someone who acted as guardian for friends' offspring, distributed money to needy companions, and loved telling a good yarn.

Well known, entertaining, genial, and popular, Pete was also broke when he died. So the Society of Arizona Pioneers stepped in and paid the $40 cost of his funeral. After all, the *Citizen* pointed out, Pete Kitchen was a legend, "one of the most remarkable men that ever faced the frontier dangers of the far southwest."

During the course of his life, Pete Kitchen literally followed the ever-moving frontier. He was, in every respect, a product of the nation's faith in its own Manifest Destiny.

Born in 1819 near Covington, Kentucky, and raised in Tennessee, Pete worked in Texas with the U.S. Army as a teamster and wagonmaster during the Mexican War. There, he probably acquired his fluency in Spanish and fondness for wearing a Mexican poncho and big sombrero. After the war, Pete went to Fort Leavenworth, in what is now Kansas, and signed on with a military wagon train bound for Fort Vancouver, Oregon.

Upon reaching the West Coast Pete headed straight for California where, along with hordes of other forty-niners bent on "seeing the elephant," he joined in the great gold rush. He evidently fared no better than most prospectors, for the real money to be made in California lay not in panning for gold but in providing miners with whatever goods and services they required. In 1854, he followed the frontier to Tucson, as southern Arizona below the Gila River had been acquired by the U.S. that year through the Gadsden Purchase.

Pete's arrival in Tucson coincided with an economic boom in southern Arizona. American miners, like most folks, viewed Hispanic Arizona as a land of mystery and hidden wealth. Spurred on by tales of lost Jesuit treasure and mountains of silver, they swarmed across the country-side, secure in the belief that the Gadsden Purchase presented them with a key for opening up untapped riches. To protect its adventurous citizens from Apache raiders, the Army established a chain of forts in the region. Pete, sensing opportunity, set himself up with a herd of cattle along the Santa Cruz River, about 25 miles south of Tucson. He still dabbled in mining but, having learned the lessons of the California gold rush, relied mainly on providing others with the products of pasture and field.

Unfortunately for Pete, this pastoral existence did not last long.

Apache attacks, long a regular feature of life in the Santa Cruz Valley, took an especially ferocious turn in 1861. Troops parleying at Apache Pass with Chiricahua chief Cochise about a boy kidnapped from his family's ranch hanged six Apache hostages. The Apaches responded in kind, with interest, burning ranches, stealing horses, running off stock, and killing travelers. One day Pete returned from delivering a consignment of beef to Fort Buchanan and found Apache warriors had paid him a visit, torching his ranch and making off with 440 horses and cattle.

Things got even worse in the spring of 1861, when the Civil War erupted and soldiers withdrew for battles in the East, leaving southern Arizona unprotected. Pete wisely made his way to Magdalena, Sonora, Mexico about 60 miles below the border. The international boundary in those days was unfenced and people constantly drifted back and forth. Southern Arizona and northern Sonora enjoyed much in the way of shared

experiences and customs. Indeed, a common, bilingual frontier borderland culture eventually emerged.

Pete spent seven years in Magdalena, where he operated a store with a woman named Rosa Verdugo. Then, in 1868, Pete returned to Arizona, accompanied by Rosa and their two-year-old son, Santiago (James), as well as a large retinue: Rosa's brother Francisco Verdugo; her sister, and brother-in-law Manuel Ronquillo; their families; and possibly as many as 30 Opata Indians. On a creek, near its junction with the Santa Cruz about five miles north from where the twin cities of Nogales sprawl across the border today, Pete claimed squatter's rights. He called his ranch El Potrero (The Pasture), the same name by which the creek became known.

In the fertile flatlands stretching out north and south, Pete's outfit drained swamps and dug irrigation ditches to nourish crops of corn, barley, potatoes, cabbages, and melons. Cattle and horses grazed on the tall grass covering the hills rising up in the east and west. Along the creek, Pete set a herd of pigs roaming, which he butchered for hams and sausages. On a rise above Potrero Creek's west bank, Pete and his *compañeros* built the main ranch house, a single-story, 12-foot-tall, L-shaped, 60-foot-long adobe structure known as "The Stronghold." A well, combined with a walled-in complex containing quarters for ranch hands, corrals, smokehouse, and general store, proclaimed self-sufficiency and safety.

John G. Bourke, an Army officer who served in Arizona during the Apache wars, left an account of a visit to El Potrero, "which has all the airs of a feudal castle in the days of chivalry." According to Bourke, "Within the hospitable walls of the Kitchen home the traveler was made to feel perfectly at ease. If food were not already on the fire, some of the women set about the preparation of the savory and spicy stews for which the Mexicans are deservedly famous, and others kneaded the dough and patted into shape the paper-like tortillas with which to eat the juicy frijoles [beans] or dip up the tempting chile colorado [red chile]. There were women carding, spinning, sewing — doing the thousand and one duties of domestic life in a great ranch, which had its own blacksmith, saddler, and wagonmaker, and all other officials needed to keep the machinery running smoothly."

But this idyllic atmosphere proved tragically deceptive, for Pete's ranch straddled a north-south raiding route long followed by Apaches.

This is why, as he approached The Stronghold, John Bourke spied a sentry posted on top of the ranch house's flat roof, protected by a four-foot-tall parapet dotted with firing portals; another guard covered the stock corralled in a nearby gully. Men working in the fields "are obliged to carry rifles, cocked and loaded, swung to the plough handles." Weapons abounded at El Potrero: "Every man and boy is armed with one or two revolvers on the hip. There are revolvers and rifles and shotguns along the walls and in every corner. Everything speaks of a land of warfare and bloodshed."

Indeed, El Potrero's residents constantly faced danger. Consider some of the comings-and-goings of early 1869. The new year was only 18 days old when Apaches made off with 17 of Pete's horses. Less than three weeks later, a Mexican shepherd appeared at the ranch with news that Apaches had stolen his flock. Pete and some of the hands rode off in pursuit, chased the Apaches away, counted 250 butchered sheep, and drove the remaining animals back to El Potrero. There, Pete learned that a neighbor off deer hunting never returned home. The next morning, Pete searched for his friend and found him lying dead in a nearby canyon, killed by Apaches.

Other episodes speak of the precarious quality of life in Pete Kitchen's world. Riding along one day, one of his employees, an African-American cowboy known only as Henry, felt a rope's noose drop over his shoulders as he passed under a tree. Responding with lightning quickness, Henry spurred his horse into a gallop, yanked hard on the rope, and knifed the Apache holding the other end.

John Bourke did not overstate matters when he reported that "ceaseless war" took place between Pete and the Apaches: "His employees were killed and wounded, his stock driven away, his pigs filled with arrows, making the suffering quadrupeds look like perambulating pin-cushions

— everything that could be thought of to drive him away but there he stayed, unconquered and unconquerable." In fact, the road between Tucson and Pete's place, which passed by the ruined presidio at Tubac and the abandoned mission at Tumacacori, was so insecure that he and others grimly bestowed a new name on the route: "To-son, To-bac, To-macacori, To-Hell!"

Perhaps the most oft-told tale of Pete's days at El Potrero involves a spectacular feat of marksmanship. One day an Apache sniper took up a position behind a large boulder at the top of a hill some 500 yards east of Pete's home. In those days single-shot rifles were common and shooters needed time to reload after firing their weapons. So Pete told Rosa to fire at the sniper, who immediately ducked behind the rock. Then, believing himself safe, the Apache stuck his head out for a peek, whereupon Pete cut lose with a single, fatal shot. The story is very likely true, but other episodes from Pete Kitchen's life remain a bit more mythic.

Back in 1958, Gil Procter, who for many years owned Pete's ranch and operated a museum at the site, published a little book called *People of the Moonlight*. In this whimsical volume, Procter related a tale about how Pete saved the life of a famed Apache's child in August, 1873. Pete and his comrade, Pancho, were riding along the bed of the Santa Cruz River when Pete heard someone singing an Apache death song. He and Pancho quickly discovered half a dozen members of "the Chavez gang," torturing a teenaged Apache boy. Getting the drop on these villains, Pete rescued the Apache, who turned out to be Cochise's son, Chise. (In fact, Cochise apparently never had a son of that name; perhaps Procter meant Naiche, born in 1856.)

Loading the boy onto a horse, Pete and Pancho took him to the safety of El Potrero, where Rosa nursed him back to health. "I think this means the end of our war with Cochise," Pete confided to his family at dinner that night. Later, after Chise returned to his father, Cochise and Pete met in Sulphur Springs Valley, smoked cigarettes together, and pledged eternal peace.

The story, however charming, is almost certainly apocryphal — like the one about Apaches killing young Santiago Kitchen within sight of The Stronghold — but it shows just how easily Pete Kitchen's life lends itself to the stuff of legend.

Although a perilous undertaking, Pete often visited Tucson, capital of Arizona Territory from 1867 to 1877. The 60-mile journey from El Potrero took several days and required careful preparations. Piling hams, potatoes, other salable crops, and supplies into slow-moving, two-wheeled Mexican carts called *carretas*, Pete protected the members of his extended family who accompanied him by building up grain-sack barricades around the wagon beds.

Tucson represented civilization, or as close to it as Pete would ever get, though the town also displayed its fair share of rough edges. San Francisco-based journalist J. Ross Browne, visiting Tucson a few years earlier, described it as "quite a place of resort for traders, speculators, gamblers, horse-thieves, murderers, and vagrant politicians." John G. Bourke remembered the Tucson he and Pete knew in the 1870s. Of paved streets, "there were none; lamps were unheard of; drainage was not deemed necessary. . . . There was no hint in history or tradition of a sweeping of the streets, which were every bit as filthy as those of New York." Nevertheless, Pete and Rosa could dine in the famed Shoo Fly restaurant — so named because, locals claimed, "the flies wouldn't shoo worth a cent" — where a sign proclaimed: "All meals payable in advance."

In Pete's time, Tucsonans rarely spoke of days, weeks, or months, preferring to reckon time's passage by pegging it to recollections of well-known events. Sometimes it was, "Jes' about th' time Pete Kitchen's ranch was jumped," though John Bourke found this unsatisfactorily imprecise, "as Pete Kitchen's ranch was always getting 'jumped.'"

Apache raiders struck at El Potrero for the last time in the spring of 1877. But nettling sources of trouble remained. Early in 1879, a band of Mexican outlaws appeared along the Santa Cruz. Pete sent a vaquero to Magdalena, requesting that local authorities ride north and position themselves on a rise above the spot where the Santa Cruz leaves Mexico. Meanwhile, Pete led a group of horsemen in an encircling maneuver along the sides of the valley, driving the bandits before them toward the border. Upon entering Mexico the *bandidos* fell into the hands of waiting lawmen, who summarily shot them.

By then, the frontier was closing down for good. El Potrero's *campo santo*, its burial ground, remained a reminder of Pete's friends and family who lost their lives defending the place they called home. Outside the stubby rock walls of the cemetery lay the graves of Apaches killed by Pete and his *compadres*, men who also died defending their homes. But now, five miles south of El Potrero, the town of Nogales, then called Isaacson by some and Line City by others, took shape. In 1882 railroad surveyors showed up at Pete's ranch, laying out a route along a Benson-Calabasas-Nogales line in an effort to link up with the Mexican seaport at Guaymas. Within months, trains arrived at Calabasas. For Pete, who came to the valley as a squatter and thought of his land as extending "as far as you find a horse with my brand," the Pima County Commissioners' condemnation of a right-of-way across his ranch must have come as quite a shock.

Then, it was over. In 1883 Pete sold El Potrero for $5,000 and moved to Tucson, where he spent the remaining dozen years of his life. There, living in a house on Main Street with Rosa — she would survive him by some years and end her days at Sacaton — Pete must have wondered what life was all about as he watched various real estate and ranching ventures go bust. His mining endeavors north and south of the Mexican border were widely thought of as notorious failures. In fact, the result of one prospecting trip into Sonora — we lack details, but Pete evidently nearly lost his life — inspired a well-known Arizona one-liner, with pioneers referring to unlucky acquaintances as "getting what Pete Kitchen got in Sonora." If the money disappeared and some personal relations soured — Pete and his son Santiago drew apart — Kitchen at least enjoyed the acclaim of those who shared Arizona's frontier experience.

People typically recall pioneer Kentucky's famed "Dark and Bloody Ground" as a model for the horrors of frontier warfare. But as John Bourke observed, "Kentucky never was anything except a Sunday-school convention in comparison with Arizona, every mile of whose surface could tell its tale of horror were the stones and gravel, the sage-brush and mescal, the mesquite and the yucca, only endowed with speech for one brief hour."

In 1891, a generation after first meeting Pete

Kitchen, John Bourke looked back on those frontier days and his friend. Arizona, he recalled, had been "full of such people, not all as determined and resolute as Pete . . . but all with histories full of romance and excitement." Now, he noted with regret, few of them remained "and their deeds of heroism will soon be forgotten, or, worse luck yet, some of the people who never dreamed of going down there until they could do so in a Pullman car will be setting themselves up as heroes, and having their puny biographies written for the benefit of the coming generations."

A child of the frontier — moving with it through the Mexican War to the Pacific Coast, into the California gold rush, and on to Arizona and to northern Mexico — Pete Kitchen passed on as that frontier also disappeared. The image of a frontiersman locked in a deadly contest with Apaches is no longer seen as the good-versus-evil struggle it appeared to be in Kitchen's time. Today, we detect subtler nuances and the equation seems more complex. Nevertheless, Pete Kitchen's is a story that speaks volumes about how residents of the territory perceived themselves and their time and how they viewed Arizona's frontier experience.

Today Pete Kitchen's grave is lost somewhere beneath the bustling Tucson metropolis. Truly, though, Pete Kitchen needs no granite marker to stand as a reminder that he once lived in the valley marked by the signposts of its destinations: "To-son, To-bac, To-macacori, To-Hell!" That's why the Society of Arizona Pioneers paid for his funeral.

In this one detects the kind of irony Pete would surely have enjoyed. For soon after joining that organization in

1884, Pete, finding himself in arrears for dues, requested that his name be "raced of the Rowl." But, as his admirers knew when joining together for the last time to honor him, Pete Kitchen's name could never be erased from the roll of Arizona's pioneers.

CHAPTER ELEVEN

James Ohio Pattie

*Mountain man James Ohio Pattie was among
the first white men in the American Southwest
in the 1820s. His recollections, dictated and
published upon his return to Kentucky, likely
exaggerated his adventures but painted
a vivid picture of the country and the people
for generations of readers.*

BY DEAN SMITH

⟫——◆——⟪

I T WAS THE LURE OF BEAVER FURS THAT BROUGHT YOUNG
James Ohio Pattie and his adventurous companions to
what is now southern Arizona in 1825. The Gila River
and its tributaries flowed through a pristine wilderness —
a Garden of Eden without a single white man's settlement
or even a wagon track. Bears and deer roamed the forested
hills, and wild turkeys abounded. In emerald glades, grass
grew as high as a horse's shoulder. And there were beavers
— tens of thousands of them — busily gnawing down willows and cottonwoods along the crystal streams to build
their dams and lodges.

This land was technically a part of Mexico, only
recently liberated from Spanish rule, but in fact it was the
uncontested domain of Indian tribes who never before had
been forced to share it with white men and were fiercely
determined to keep them out. The warriors ran off the
trappers' horses, stole their furs, and sometimes roasted

dismembered American bodies over their campfires.

Venturing into this beautiful but deadly wilderness took courage of the highest order. This the buckskin-clad mountain men had in great abundance. Before he had completed his amazing five-year odyssey, Pattie (according to the memoirs he dictated on his return to Kentucky) had battled a bear in a pitch-black cave, rescued the beautiful daughter of a former Mexican governor, saved the lives of several thousand Californians by inoculating them against small pox, cheated death many times, and killed dozens of Indians.

Historians, for more than 160 years, have been dissecting and criticizing Pattie's narrative, which was edited by Rev. Timothy Flint of Cincinnati in 1831 and became an instant best-seller. There is general agreement that Pattie may have exaggerated his exploits just a bit — probably a lot. But there is little doubt that he was in the first American party to cross Arizona to the Colorado River and live to tell the tale.

His book, *The Personal Narrative of James Ohio Pattie of Kentucky,* remains today as an invaluable record of what Arizona was like two decades before Mexico ceded our present Southwest to the United States.

One mystery about that document remains: why Pattie never identified the leaders of any of the trapping parties in which he traveled, except for his father in one venture. Historians, however, have been able to piece together information that places him in the expeditions led by Miguel Robidoux and Ewing Young, two of the most famous mountain men.

Pattie was a minor character in the saga of the beaver trappers. Heroic figures such as Young, Bill Williams,

George Yount, Paulino Weaver, Robidoux, and Kit Carson accomplished more and probably endured more hardships than he. But they left only fragmentary records, or none at all.

Pattie's place in history has been assured, as is so often the case, because he took the trouble to record his adventures for posterity.

No gentleman on either side of the Atlantic would have been without a high-crowned beaver hat in the 1820s. The resulting demand for beaver pelts created such a lucrative market that many hundreds of rugged adventurers were willing to risk death at the hands of hostile Indians and the cruel elements to trap the wily little dam builders in the rivers of the West.

The beaver rush, which rivaled the gold rush of later years, came perilously close to trapping these animals to extinction in less than a decade. But the species survived, and today beavers may be found in many Arizona rivers and lakes, especially in White Mountain streams and the Colorado River. In fact, beavers are considered pests in some areas because they strip the bark from fruit trees and dam up irrigation canals.

The trappers of the mid-1820s could harvest beavers only during Arizona's cooler months because the animals shed much of their lustrous brown fur in hot weather. Traps were anchored to a five-foot chain near the stream bank and baited with beaver musk. When the beaver came to investigate, the trap was sprung and the frightened victim tried to escape by diving into deeper water, only to die by drowning.

The beaver, weighing from 30 to 60 pounds and with

a flat tail that was considered a culinary delicacy, was skinned and the pelt scraped, dried, and packed with other furs into a bale of about a hundred pounds, which was then loaded onto a pack animal.

If sold at a mountain trading post, a pelt weighing two pounds was worth six to eight dollars. If the trapper could get his furs through Indian country and back to St. Louis, he would be paid at least half again as much. It was possible for a trapping party to cash in for as much as $10,000 — enough to keep its members in some luxury for years.

James Ohio Pattie, age 20, came west from Kentucky in 1824 with his father, Sylvester, in search of adventure and a quick fortune. In Santa Fe they joined a trapping party being organized by Sylvester Pratte, which was about to venture into the virtually unmapped Gila River country. But the expedition was halted by the Mexican governor, who would not issue them a trapping license.

Fate stepped in when a Comanche band raided a nearby settlement and carried off five women, including the beautiful young daughter of a former Mexican governor. Pattie and several others volunteered to rescue them. In Pattie's words:

> We waited in ambush and soon saw five women, without clothes, driving sheep and horses. These were immediately followed by Indians. When the latter were within thirty yards of us we fired and the women ran toward us. Three of them were killed by Indian spears, but a young man and myself sprang forward and rescued the remaining two. . . . We wrapped them in blankets and returned to our post.

One of the two was Jacova, the ex-governor's daughter. Her father was so grateful that he arranged for the trappers to get their license. And so the great adventure began.

James called the river the "Helay" and used semi-phonetic spelling for most other place names and Indian tribes, such as Ymus (Guaymas); the Papawar (Papago), Nabahoe (Navaho), and Mokee (Moqui, or Hopi). But his descriptions of Arizona geography are remarkably accurate.

Arriving on the Gila in December, 1824, the party caught 30 beavers the first time they set their traps. They crossed into today's Arizona in early January, 1825, and followed the Gila to the San Francisco River. Passing the site of modern Clifton, they trapped the San Francisco to its source, harvesting 250 more pelts. Most of these they had to bury for later recovery because their horses were already overloaded.

It was at this time that Pattie claimed to pursue a bear into its cave, placing a lighted torch alongside his rifle to pierce the blackness.

Then, I advanced through the black cave some 20 yards. Of a sudden, the bear reared himself erect within seven feet of me and began to growl and gnash his teeth. I leveled my gun and shot him between the eyes. Then I ran, dropping my torch and gun in my retreat. When I returned, I found the great animal dead, much to my relief.

The party pressed on, and soon had to leave the Gila

because of an impassable canyon. But shortly they were able to return to the stream and found virgin beaver country. Within a few days they had 200 more pelts, which they again cached in a hiding place. But soon a band of Indian raiders (probably Apaches) ran off their horses, leaving them to make their way back to New Mexico on foot.

Acquiring more horses, they returned to their two caches of buried furs, only to find that Indians had stolen the latter one. But the San Francisco River furs were intact, and they were sold in Santa Fe for $1,200.

After a rest of several months, James joined the Miguel Robidoux party of French trappers. This group of some 30 men had more ambitious plans: trapping the Gila and any tributaries they might find, all the way to the Colorado River (Pattie called it the "Red" and the Salt River the "Black").

Arriving in Arizona in January, 1826, they fought off several Indian attacks in their westward push. They passed just south of today's Chandler and Phoenix, reaching a village of Maricopa Indians near the confluence of the Gila and Salt. Because the natives seemed friendly, the French trappers accepted their invitation to spend the night in their village. Pattie and several others, however, were suspicious and made camp some distance away. About midnight, Pattie heard war cries, screams, and groans coming from the village and escaped with his contingent to "a high mountain on the south side of the river" eluding the pursuing warriors. Only the French leader, Robidoux, survived and made his way, severely wounded, to rejoin Pattie's band.

As if by a miracle, Ewing Young's trappers appeared on the scene a few hours later, and the combined force of

26 men launched a revenge attack on the Maricopa village. According to Pattie, the Indians "paid a bloody price for their treachery . . . for 110 of them were slain."

After trapping up the Salt and Verde rivers, the men made their way westward along the Gila, suffering greatly from hunger and heat until they reached the Colorado River at the site of present-day Yuma.

Pattie described the Yumas (Umene, he called them) as "men of the finest forms I ever saw, six to seven feet tall, straight as an arrow . . . They flatten their heads by pressing a board upon the children's tender scalps."

The party turned north up the Colorado, enjoying excellent beaver trapping much of the way. But at the mouth of a tributary later named for Bill Williams they encountered savage Indians who killed three of their party, cut their bodies in pieces, and roasted them over a fire.

On they went, soon entering the Grand Canyon. Before this epic four-month trek ended back at Santa Fe, the Ewing Young trappers had explored parts of Utah, Colorado, and Nevada, exploring 2,100 miles of wilderness. Almost a third of their party had been killed by Indians.

They returned with about $20,000 worth of furs, only to have the Mexican governor, Don Manuel Armijo, confiscate them because he claimed they did not have a valid license. Once more, Pattie and his mates had risked death and suffered privation for virtually no reward.

It is not hard to imagine how trappers looked — and smelled — after such a sojourn in the wild. Historian Robert Cleland described them as having skin "as dark as the aborigines, with long, dirty hair." Their clothing was of buckskin, with fur hat and footwear of deer or other tough hide. Most wore a deerskin overshirt which, when soaked repeatedly in water, dried as hard as mail, "turning away all but the hardest-driven arrows."

Trappers, says Cleland, commonly carried a rifle and packed about 100 flints, 25 pounds of powder, 100 pounds of lead, powder horn, skinning knife, hatchet, and four to six traps. Food and drink were provided by the land through which they passed.

In the autumn of 1827, both James Pattie and his father joined another party headed for the Colorado. He tells how the Cocopahs south of Yuma gave them a feast of roast dog, after which the chief brought in naked Indian girls, "no more than 16 years of age. We passed the night most pleasantly with them, to the satisfaction of all parties."

Beaver trapping, it seems, was not all pain and hardship.

The party split there, and the Patties trapped to the mouth of the Colorado, buried their furs, and headed for the village of San Diego, almost dying of thirst crossing the burning desert. When they arrived, the Mexican governor, Jose Maria Encheandia, branded them as spies, tore up their passports, and clapped them all into jail.

Ill and weak from his desert nightmare, the elder Pattie died in his cell a few weeks later. James was imprisoned for several months and was released only because he offered to halt a smallpox epidemic that was sweeping the California coast. In his memoir, he claimed to have found in his late father's baggage a quantity of smallpox vaccine. With it, and other vaccines which he later acquired, he inoculated 22,000 Mexicans and Indians over a period of several months and saved their communities from certain death.

Free at last, Pattie headed homeward, but only after

journeying to Mexico City to plead, unsuccessfully, for payment due him for the loss of his furs, for his false imprisonment, and for saving the Californians from smallpox.

He arrived back in Kentucky in early 1830, nearly penniless, broken in body and spirit, and thoroughly disillusioned. In the epilog to his memoir, he declared sadly:

"The freshness, the visions, the hopes of my youthful days are all vanished and can never return. If there is a lesson in my wanderings, it is that of remaining at the paternal home in peace and privacy, and not to wander far away to see the habitations and endure the inhospitality of strangers."

Although demoralized after his adventures, perhaps he would have taken solace if he could have known that his memoirs would still be read and pondered more than a century and a half later and that he had indeed left his mark on the history of Arizona and the Southwest.

C. Hart Merriam

*Although trained as a physician, Merriam's first
love was natural history, and he quit his
medical practice to head what was to become the
U.S. Department of Agriculture's Biological
Survey. His research in the late 1880s took
him to the wilds of northern Arizona where he
developed his landmark theory of "life zones."*

B Y   K A Y   J O R D A N   W H I T H A M

———◆———

T HEY HAD RUN OUT OF WATER. AND AFTER A DAY OF TRAV-
eling through the unrelenting August heat of the
Painted Desert without it, naturalist C. Hart
Merriam halted his expedition in a sliver of shade, looking
from his map to the surrounding cliffs in search of a landmark or a glimmer of green that would guide them to the
precious fluid. But all he saw were dry cliffs, "burning sand
. . . and the intense heat, from which there is no escape."

His wife, Elizabeth, suffering with painfully parched
lips, dabbed ointment while packer W.W. Stout tried to
soothe the flagging burros loaded with biological survey
gear. Merriam retraced on the map their route across the
desert. That was the only alternative now, to return to base
camp at Little Springs by the route they came. But could
they do it?

The previous day, August 14, 1889, the Merriams,
Stout, and the mules crossed the summer-dry Little

Colorado River at Grand Falls and headed up Dinnebito Wash, leaving behind Vernon Bailey, Merriam's assistant, at base camp.

Merriam's journal entry for that day read: "It was terribly hot and there was no water . . . save an occasional pool of alkaline mud from which we could skim off a cup part full of water. The ther. stood at 113 degrees Fahr. at the height of one's head [in shade]. I put it down in the sun, and it ran up instantly . . . the full length of the tube."

Night brought little respite. First, a fierce wind sandblasted camp, then a flash flood "rushed past with a tremendous roar accompanied by a fetid stench." Finally, "ants were so abundant we could not sleep, so we moved our blankets but still they crawled over our faces by thousands." After four hours of restless tossing, the party started hunting for the sole source of water in the area: Dinnebito Spring, which they never found.

Clinton Hart Merriam, one of America's great naturalists, came to Arizona to learn why plants and animals live where they do, which eventually led him to the creation of "life zones" for North America, which brought praise but also provided fuel for critics.

Although trained as a physician, his first love was natural history, and in the course of his life he identified a number of species of mammals and birds, among which the Merriam elk and turkey are the best known. In 1885, Merriam, then 30, quit his practice to head what was to become the U.S. Department of Agriculture's Biological Survey. There he persuaded his superiors he could solve the riddle of plant and animal distribution if allowed to study a remote mountain region with different climates and a variety of animal and vegetable life. Granted two months' leave and $600, Merriam set off with his assistant and his wife on a journey to northern Arizona.

On this scorching August day in the Painted Desert, however, Merriam's first concern was not science but survival. Without water, they knew, they couldn't go on. In desperation, he sent his packer, Stout, up into the cliffs to make a search. Hours later, Stout found water, but so little, Merriam recorded, "the only way in the world I could get it up was to suck it up into my mouth and then spit it out . . ." He nearly half-filled a small canteen "and we completely emptied it . . . knowing *exactly* how it had been procured."

Despite thirst and heat, Merriam somehow managed to continue the survey. He crossed the desert, collecting cactuses, reptiles, and rodents. He saw burrowing owls, but, to his disappointment, never spotted a road runner. He also observed that as he traveled up the desert canyons to the mountain slopes, it became cooler and wetter. This, he believed, confirmed his hypothesis that temperature was the critical factor in determining plant and animal distribution. Humidity played an important secondary role. Today, these two variables are still considered crucial to plant and animal distribution, but their effects are more complex than Merriam imagined.

Near collapse, the party arrived at last at the Little Springs base camp 18 miles northwest of Flagstaff, where Merriam and assistant Vernon Bailey skinned and mounted the birds and mammals collected and recorded where each had been found. The techniques they used had been developed by Merriam, who was trained in taxidermy and, at age 16, had secured the post of naturalist for the 1871 Hayden

Expedition to Yellowstone, Wyoming. Later he collected in Maine, Florida, Bermuda, and Greenland. As chief of the Biological Survey, Merriam combined his knowledge of taxidermy with his field experience to standardize methods of animal preservation. This greatly expanded the knowledge about birds and mammals, since specimens collected at different times and places by numerous collectors could now be compared.

Although Merriam earned a reputation as a demanding taskmaster, he and Bailey worked well together. Bailey accommodated Merriam's exacting standards, and Merriam respected his assistant's refusal to work on Sundays. Eight years younger than Merriam, Bailey described his stout mustachioed boss as "a queer old chap, but a splendid fellow to camp with, always does his share and never shirks the dirty or hard work."

Botanist F.H. Knowlton and reptile specialist Leonard Stejneger joined the expedition later, with Knowlton arriving while Merriam was in the Painted Desert. Stejneger, who came to Arizona for his health, was so ill, Merriam was certain he would die while on the survey. From their camp of tents, the naturalists traveled on horseback to Kendrick Peak, Walnut Canyon, once more to the Painted Desert, and up the slopes of the San Francisco Mountains. Everywhere they went, they collected plants, trapped or shot animals, mapped the distribution of trees, and recorded altitude, temperature, and rainfall.

Not all the animals shot were for science; some were for supper. "I killed a big golden eagle. It measured 7 feet 2 inches across . . . ." Bailey wrote, adding, "It wasn't bad eating." Some meals didn't meet with universal approval. When mountain lion was served, Bailey complained,

"[Merriam] says it is delicious, but it is horribly catty. I can't eat it and Knowlton won't." Of the skunk Merriam cooked, Bailey said flatly, "I couldn't help him eat it."

As the naturalists surveyed northern Arizona, Merriam noticed that vegetation formed concentric rings around the mountain and certain plants and animals were characteristic of each ring. In the Painted Desert he collected drought-adapted plants, lizards, and nocturnal rodents, but at slightly higher elevations he observed piñon jays feeding on the nut-like piñon pine seeds. Below Little Springs, he saw vast stands of ponderosa pine inhabited by tufted-eared squirrels and "handsome horned toads," and on the mountain summit he encountered birds and low-growing plants similar to those he'd seen in the Arctic. He realized that within these concentric zones there were distinct communities of plants and animals dependent upon one another. This led Merriam to "unexpected generalizations" that helped lay the foundation for a new biological science.

In September the expedition took a long-anticipated collecting trip to the Grand Canyon, which turned into more of an adventure than Merriam had planned on. Taking along some traps, a bag of pancakes, and guns Merriam and Bailey started down the canyon.

Halfway down, Merriam sprained his knee and was forced to stop while Bailey went on. After resting a day, Merriam started to hike back to the rim alone, dragging his lame leg.

"Everything is merged into one gigantic, vertical black wall which encloses the spectator and seems to reach the sky," Merriam wrote about his climb to the Rim. "The moon and stars shone brightly and enabled me to pick my way along the bottom of the canyon, but the walls were black and often cast heavy shadows across my path. A hundred times they seemed to meet and shut me in without the possibility of escape, a hundred times the rounding of a curve or the passing of a projecting cliff extended the limits of my prison. The way seemed without end." At dawn Merriam finally crested the Canyon rim.

After a second collecting trip to the Painted Desert, where Bailey observed: "Green seems to be the only color wanting," the expedition disbanded, and Merriam returned to Washington to write "Results of a Biological Survey of the San Francisco Mountain Region and Desert of the Little Colorado."

In his report Merriam organized the rings of interdependent plants and animals observed into seven distinct communities or, as he called them, "life zones." Each zone was characterized by a unique suite of plants and animals, and because of the effects of temperature and humidity, each was limited to a specific elevational range. They began with the Timberline, Spruce, Douglas Fir, Pine, Piñon, and Desert zones.

Then, comparing the hotter, drier conditions he encountered when traveling down the mountain to the same pattern he noted when journeying from north to south, Merriam expanded his Arizona life zones to all of North America. (This extension proved inaccurate, and today a modified version of the zones is used only in the West and Southwest.) Remembering his study was funded and published by the Agriculture Department, Merriam recommended crops for those zones suited for farming.

Although his life zones concept opened new fields of biological study, the report also provided fuel for Merriam's critics. The Biological Survey was charged with studying birds and animals with little economic value. This broader scope allowed him to develop his life zones, but his superiors and Congress demanded results with immediate agriculture impact. In 1910, tired of defending his work, he retired from government service and spent the remainder of his life studying obscure California Indian tribes. He died in 1942.

Unfortunately, C. Hart Merriam did not solve the riddle of plant and animal distribution as he planned, but his Arizona study was valuable nevertheless — not in the answers it provided, but in the questions it raised. The idea of combining plants and animals in life zones was so intriguing it demanded further study. Even biologists who disagreed with Merriam felt compelled to test his theories in order to devise better explanations, and new lines of research were begun which continue to this day in botany, forestry, mammalogy, and biogeography. The principle underlying life zones — that plants, animals, and their environment are interdependent — eventually became a cornerstone of ecology, a cornerstone cut from the mountains of Arizona by pioneer naturalist C. Hart Merriam.

Sylvester Mowry

*Dashing Army officer, successful mine owner,
unprincipled lady's man, duelist, and convicted
Confederate sympathizer, Sylvester Mowry
also was an ardent and effective promoter whose
efforts were instrumental in the creation
of the Territory of Arizona.*

B Y   T I M   V A N D E R P O O L

━━━◆◆◆━━━

THE WIND WAS HOWLING AS SYLVESTER MOWRY SPUN clockwise and squeezed off three shots from his Burnside rifle. Eighty paces away, newspaperman Edward Cross returned fire. But Cross was an editor, not a marksman, and suddenly regretted he'd spent all his fire-power in four quick jerks. His opponent now eyed him through the gunsmoke. Mowry remained unscathed, except for the dust in his beard: a single bullet remained chambered in his rifle.

Spectators clamoring on either side of the field grew silent. Mostly gamblers and miners, they'd wagered heavily on this duel in the desert south of Tucson. Nervously they whispered, and wondered: would Mowry, the fiery second lieutenant, successful mine owner, infamous Casanova, and tireless Arizona promoter, gun down his helpless quarry?

Most considered the duel inevitable. After all, Mowry was a well-known blowhard. To spellbound Easterners, the tall, handsome officer had passionately described Arizona as an untapped verdant paradise — its forests full, its rivers thick with oversized fish. His inflated population numbers turned up in official documents, even in President Buchanan's speeches to Congress.

And Cross, indignant as a startled viper, had fired several biting missives to the St. Louis' *Missouri Republican* under the pseudonym "Gila." He cited "an enormous amount of falsehood published concerning the country and its resources." As editor of Tubac's *Weekly Arizonian,* Cross reported seeing few fish, and none bigger than his fingernail. These he called "Mowry Trout."

The lieutenant stuck by his claims. "I assert it," he responded, "and have proved it by more evidence that it would be sufficient to hang 20 such fellows as the writer of this anonymous letter if he was on trial — a fate, by the way, which will be apt to overtake him when his letter goes back to Arizona."

An indignant Mowry finally called Cross on his words, challenging him to a duel. It culminated on July 8, 1859. As a motley gallery watched, the two rivals faced one another. Resigned to fate, Cross bravely stood his ground, arms folded. But whatever else Mowry might be, he was a gentleman, and his fourth shot went deliberately high.

Mowry had taken the noble route. The match was called a draw, and alongside a 42-gallon barrel of prime Monongahela whiskey, sore points were soon guzzled away. Another episode in the rambunctious story of Sylvester Mowry — one inextricably linked with frontier Arizona — had come to a friendly end. He subsequently bought Cross' paper and moved it to Tucson. There it would trumpet the area's territorial ambitions and his own budding silver fortunes.

By 1861 the Mowry Mine worked over 100 men and shipped out $700 daily in ore. It boasted a smelter, furnaces, and deep, rich shafts. Less than a morning's ride from the Mexican border, near present-day Patagonia, it was also a prime target for marauding Indians and Mexican bandits.

Government troops had become scarce, drawn east to the impending Civil War. Many settlers followed suit, packing out in droves. Not Mowry. Instead, he turned his outpost into a fortress and pleaded for military protection.

Today, leaves scuttle across the decaying settlement. Oak-studded hillsides are spread with reddish tailings and pierced by a scattering of ominous fenced-in shafts. Sleeping quarters and offices have crumbled to remnants of adobe walls and masonry foundations. Lizards glide among rusty artifacts.

It's serene there, that bittersweet quiet of ghost towns. But as it surrenders to silence, Mowry, Arizona, still reveals the gutsy ambition of its namesake.

Born in 1832, Sylvester Mowry grew up in Rhode Island, was graduated from West Point, and landed in Salt Lake City. There he was assigned to the Northern Pacific Railroad Exploring Expedition. Within weeks his unit would forge a military route to southern California. Meanwhile Mowry was charting his own lustful path, leading to Brigham Young's daughter-in-law.

Mary Young was sexy, gracious, and charming. She also was married. That apparently didn't matter to Mowry, who told friends he'd been meeting her secretly for months while her husband was on a mission.

The lieutenant, however, had underestimated the Mormon zeal for moral order. When rumors about the alleged lovers began to swirl — including a snippet about them being caught in an intimate moment — Brigham Young exploded. The Army's relationship with the church was touchy anyway, and Mowry's behavior threatened a major crisis. Brigham's henchmen were talking retaliation, perhaps even murder, when the Army brass stepped in, defusing the drama by marching

their brash young officer off to the Coast.

In 1855 he was sent to Fort Yuma, at the confluence of the Gila and Colorado rivers. Letters described his post as "a hell of a place. More than 200 miles from anywhere, in the midst of Indian country — hotter than hell." Adaptable to a fault, Mowry immediately found distraction among the many Indian women in nearby camps and villages. He boasted that a bag full of beads would buy him countless nights with a dozen of them. His amorous eye eventually turned toward Mexican beauties, and one correspondence describes him eagerly awaiting his "wedding night."

"I have just got a Sonoran girl . . . for a mistress," he wrote. "She is 17, very pretty, dark hair, big black eyes, and clear olive complexion."

Those same notes also documented his more controversial affections, especially for the South and its "cherished institution." He chided a friend that, "all you Northern people put yourself in Coventry for this infernal nonsense about Kansas," where slavery status was still being decided. And he was fed up with the slavery debate. Such sentiments would soon haunt him.

In 1857 Mowry was a restless fort commander. Gripping stories of ore strikes were pouring in, and by year's end he began a series of sick leaves. Before long he was helping rich Sonorans buy up Arizona's mines and simultaneously emerging as a strong regional spokesman.

That same year, he was elected Arizona's delegate to Congress and was writing a "Memoir on the Proposed Territory of Arizona," a pamphlet devoted entirely to his newfound home. Rumors had him weighing a bid for territorial governor.

He resigned his military commission in 1858 and bought the Patagonia Mine, renaming it after himself. Several previous owners had enjoyed varying levels of success with the Patagonia, but under Mowry's hand it became truly prosperous — a short-lived proposition as national upheaval and his own ego locked onto a collision course.

When Confederate Col. John R. Baylor claimed Arizona in 1861, Mowry's loyalties were already questionable. Perhaps he was just a concerned businessman, as he argued, figuring Dixie might offer the best protection against Apache raids.

Several letters expressed this anxiety. He complained to the Department of New Mexico's commander that "we are eaten up alive by this cursed vermin. Every week they kill somebody and drive off scores of horses, mules, and cattle." Mowry's own chestnut mare now carried Cochise himself.

Capt. Sherod Hunter's Confederate rangers swept into Arizona in 1862; a few months later they evacuated rather than face Gen. James Carleton's California Column. The general wasted little time in rounding up suspected traitors, among them Sylvester Mowry.

While headquartered in California, Carleton had heard of Mowry's Confederate leanings. His suspicions were heightened when a Mowry employee accused his boss of providing ammunition to Hunter's troops. Carleton also worried that the mine, so close to the border, could become a rebel stronghold. On June 13, he assigned a detachment of troops to bring in Mowry.

A junior officer reported Mowry's arrest: "It was about 3 A.M. I found the gateway closed and fastened, but on knocking, it was at once opened by a man whom I afterward learned was the night watchman. On the gate being opened, I immediately passed through, taking with me Captain Willis and 20 men. On being admitted to the yard, I inquired of the man who opened the gate if Lieutenant Mowry was at home. He replied in the affirmative, and pointed to his bedroom door. I knocked at the door and almost immediately thereafter Mr. Mowry made his appearance in his night clothes."

The prisoner arrived in Tucson with typical flair, prompting a newspaper correspondent to note he "takes things quite coolly, puts on a good many airs; had along his mistress, private secretary and servant. I think a dose of military treatment will cure him."

Carleton quickly convened a Board of Officers to

consider the charges. Mowry admitted giving ammunition to Hunter, claiming it was to fight Indians. Far more damning were his contacts with Confederate bigwigs like Colonel Baylor, Gen. Henry Sibley, and Jefferson Davis.

"Sir: I beg to call your attention to the absolute necessity of making a display of the Confederate forces in this section of Arizona at the earliest possible moment," he wrote Baylor in 1861. "Not only on account of Indian depredations, but to inspire respect among the Mexicans on both sides of the line . . . . There is no law and order in this section, except what I preserve here — I am working about 100 men with success, and I shall be glad to welcome you or any of your representatives."

To General Sibley he confessed hearing "from emigrants that the commanding officer of the federal forces at Fort Yuma expects an attack from the Confederate forces, and has pickets established some distance above the post on the Gila River. I can learn of no movement of troops from here to California."

Detailing Union strategy sealed his fate, and in 1862 Mowry was confined to Fort Yuma — the very post he once commanded. His mine was placed in receivership. Four months later there was talk of amnesty for Arizona secessionists. Confederate troops had retreated, and there was little harm traitors could do. This mood prevailed as Mowry's case came up for review, and when the U.S. government presented no evidence against him, he was acquitted. He wasn't so lucky with his mine; no sooner was it returned than it was seized. Under the Confiscation Act — meant to punish Southern sympathizers — it was auctioned for $4,000.

Thus began Mowry's longest battle. Over the next

decade, he tapped his many government connections and undertook a nasty legal and press attack against Carleton. The general finally grew fed up. Steadfast in his judgment, he flexed his muscle as Arizona's military governor by banning Mowry from the region. "He will be arrested the moment he arrives in Arizona," Carleton ordered District Commander Col. George Bowie. "Let this be done effectually. I will not tolerate this villain's presence within my command."

Ironically, the mine still supported Mowry even as it stood idle. He retained control of it through a dummy partnership arranged in San Francisco and convinced investors it would soon disgorge incredible wealth. He was its superintendent by name only, though, and wasn't actually involved in the mine's operation beyond 1866. Nonetheless, he probably continued gathering assessments from shareholders.

Now based in New York, Mowry's attention once again turned to love, and he began dating Lillie Hitchcock, daughter of an influential San Francisco surgeon.

In 1868 he requested Lillie's hand in marriage. Her father replied with a request "that the affair may here terminate." Obviously, Dr. Hitchcock placed little stock in Mowry's claims that he was awaiting appointment as minister to Mexico.

If Hitchcock smelled a rat, his senses were correct; Mowry's impending title was pure invention. Lillie went on to marry Benjamin Howard Coit, who later immortalized her with San Francisco's Coit Tower.

Mowry returned to Arizona in 1870, apparently unfettered by Carleton. He was here to wage another bid for delegate and maybe to restore his ego, badly battered over

Lillie Hitchcock. If so, his attempts were futile. Finding no political encouragement, he threw his support behind another candidate, who was soundly trounced.

That comprised his last visit to Arizona. While hustling new investors in Washington, Mowry fell gravely ill. He recovered enough for a therapeutic junket to London, where he died on October 17, 1871. Another prominent Arizonan, Charles Poston, was by his side.

In an obituary, Poston recalled his old friend as "a man of far more than average ability, genial in disposition and liberal to a fault." The *Arizona Citizen* was not so kind: "He quit the Territory having sustained his reputation as an egotist, braggart and shameless liar."

Controversy dogged Sylvester Mowry even in death. Like many frontier mavericks, he was a study in contradictions. An arrogant cad? Sure. A thoughtless opportunist? No doubt. But he was also a natural leader with streaks of gallantry who helped put Arizona on the map. For that alone he's worth remembering.

CHAPTER FOURTEEN

James Addison Reavis

Audacious forger, expert intimidator,
and fabricator of amazing family histories,
James Addison Reavis in the late 19th century
swindled 11 million acres of the
richest land in Arizona and New Mexico

BY BJORGNE M. KEITH

I N THE 1880S AND '90S JAMES ADDISON REAVIS NEARLY pulled off the greatest land fraud in the history of the West. Through clever forgery he laid claim to a huge Spanish land grant that covered 11 million acres of some of the richest lands in Arizona and New Mexico. Then, with audacity, exceptional imagination, and simple intimidation he took advantage of the largest corporations in the region — mining companies and railroads — swindling thousands of dollars in royalties from them for their use of "his land."

Big businesses weren't his only prey. He also intimidated small ranchers and businesspeople into paying him thousands of dollars for quit claim deeds to lands they had "squatted on." For more than a decade he lived like a king on this fabulous income, then his clever scheme unraveled.

B orn in 1843 to an average family in Missouri, James Addison Reavis worked as a mule skinner as a young man. Along came the Civil War and, while serving as an enlisted man in the Confederate Army, Reavis found he had a knack for forgery. He made a tidy profit selling passes and fake requisitions, but sensing detection, the young entrepreneur deserted. He joined the Union forces, and continued his shady dealings until, once again, he made a hurried exit a few steps ahead of the law.

Back in Missouri after the war, he took a job as a conductor on a horse-drawn streetcar line. He also opened a small real estate office, eventually amassing a small fortune handling land claims, many patently dubious, but made passable with a little creative forgery. Reavis was then ready for grander schemes, and fate stepped in disguised as Dr. George Maurice Willing Jr., the black sheep of a prosperous Philadelphia family. Willing found Reavis in his St. Louis office and told him the intriguing tale of how he had met a grizzled old Mexican prospector named Peralta, down on his luck. For a mule and equipment the old man offered to trade Willing an 18th-century land grant he claimed the king of Spain had given his family. The deal was done.

Willing offered Reavis partnership if he would provide the capital and help "develop" the grant. Reavis agreed and after selling off his St. Louis holdings headed for San Francisco via Panama to pick up some additional documents. Willing traveled overland to Prescott to file on their claim to the grant.

Willing conveniently died in Prescott and Reavis managed to get possession of Willing's papers. Reavis signed the land grant over to himself and began forming his ambitious plan. He studied royal Spanish edicts, assimilating the finer points of Spanish titles and, exercising his talent for forgery, practiced the elegant calligraphy of the 18th century.

Traveling to Guadalajara and Mexico City, Reavis cultivated the state archivists. Impressed by the tall, charming American, so proud of his alleged Spanish blood and professing eagerness to help Mexican settlers regain their lands lost to the *Yanquis*, they readily gave him access to their records.

Some documents he brazenly stole from the archives. Others he doctored and salted among the genuine to be "discovered" at a later date.

With the skill of a novelist, Reavis created a family whose head he named Don Miguel Nemcic Silva de Peralta y de Cordoba.

One yellowed parchment he dated 1741 and, over the signature of King Philip V of Spain, inserted a royal edict rewarding the fictitious Don Miguel with estates in Colorado. On another, dated 1781, Reavis penned the signature of the new King Charles III, confirming the Peralta Grant and making Don Miguel the First Baron of the Colorados and a Grandee of Spain.

Returning to the States, Reavis lost no time spreading the news of his finds. In glowing terms, reporters on San Francisco newspapers wrote of James Addison Reavis and his conclusive "proof," which showed him to be the rightful owner of the Peralta Grant.

The grant Reavis claimed stretched across central Arizona and into New Mexico, measuring 225 miles long and 75 miles wide. Its boundaries ran from the confluence of the Gila and Salt rivers west of Phoenix to just east of Silver City, New Mexico, and from Four Peaks, north of Phoenix, to Picacho Pass on the south.

With his "irrefutable proof" of ownership based on a few yellowed documents, Reavis persuaded businessmen

like California million-
aire railroad magnate
Collis P. Huntington and
John W. Mackay, San
Francisco banker and
owner of Arizona's Sil-
ver King Mining Com-
pany, to pay for their
use of land on the
Peralta Grant.

Huntington handed Reavis $50,000 for the Southern
Pacific Railroad's right-of-way through the Peralta land.
John W. Mackay not only gave Reavis $25,000 outright but
was paying him a $500 monthly retainer for mining rights.
Through his agents, Reavis began collecting payment from
other businesses and settlers on the Peralta Grant. And
while there was resistance, small land owners found it
hard not to cave in to demands when they learned that railroads and mines were paying. Reavis soon was living lav-
ishly on their money.

With his ill-gotten fortune Reavis started enterprises
of his own — large lumber companies, mining ventures,
land developments, and irrigation projects. He sold stock
in these and grew even richer.

Slowly, however, public sentiment against Reavis
grew, and Reavis realized the need for stronger evidence to
bolster his claim. A living heir or heiress, a direct descen-
dant of the second Baron Peralta, had to be produced.

And produce one he did. She was Sophia Treadway, a
dressmaker in San Francisco. The illiterate daughter of an
Indian woman and a frontiersman, she was good looking,
intelligent, and pliable. He enrolled her in a convent school

where she learned to read, write, and acquire the manners necessary for the future her Svengali was planning.

Reavis traveled to Spain, and in Seville's Archives of the Indies "found" the last will of the second baron with a codicil appointing granddaughter Doña Sofia Loreta Micael Maso y Peralta his sole heir. On his death she would become Baroness de Arizonac y de los Colorados. As her husband, James assumed the title Baron de Peralta y Cordoba.

The scam worked and for almost 10 years Sofia and James lived a luxurious life as aristocrats. In March, 1893, the birth of twin sons strengthened the myth. Naming them Miguel and Carlos Jesus for the first and second barons, Reavis proudly announced that twins ran in the Peralta family.

In Arizona they built a large house with stables and servants' quarters. They maintained a mansion in Spain and an apartment in New York. In Europe they were launched on a glittering social whirl. King Alfonso XIII and Queen Maria Christina of Spain received them; Sofia was presented to Queen Victoria and was invited to the "little dinners" the Rothschilds gave for the Prince of Wales.

But the bubble ultimately burst. Back in Arizona, "Stuttering Bill" Thomas, a printer at a Florence newspaper, had a hobby of studying and collecting typefaces. He examined the Peralta documents at the courthouse in Phoenix and found damaging proof of Reavis' machinations.

One of the parchments, dated 1748, displayed a type font not invented until 1875. On others, the watermarks indicated the paper stock had been made in Minneapolis, not Spain. And the calligraphy on one 1776 document had been written with a steel pen; such pens were not in use before 1800.

Federal investigators unearthed more damning evidence and, supplied with this information, Surveyor General Royal A. Johnson of Arizona went into action. To the General Land Office in Washington, he mailed a paper titled "The Adverse Report of the Surveyor General of Arizona upon the Peralta Grant, a Complete Exposé of its Fraudulent Character."

But Reavis would not give up easily. He filed a $10 million suit against the federal government in the U.S. Court of Special Land Claims on grounds that the government had given others lands that rightfully belonged to him.

Three special federal agents dug deeper, traveling to California, Mexico, and Spain in search of more evidence. After months of arduous detective work they uncovered hundreds of documents forged by Reavis, building a strong case against the Baron of Arizona.

The trial began in June, 1896, in Santa Fe, New Mexico. Reavis, ever self-confident, made long speeches, submitted reams of documents, and presented oil paintings of Peralta ancestors, pointing out the similarities between these portraits and his twins, who were in the court room. (The paintings had been bought in Madrid's Rastro, a flea market famous as a depository of junk and antiques.)

The trial was short, and Thomas' testimony, as well as that of other expert witnesses, was devastating. They showed how strips of paper with the Peralta name and other information had been inserted in the body of authentic documents, often misspelled and in incorrect Spanish, and how, in several supposedly ancient parchments, Reavis had used type fonts made in 1885.

The evidence was undeniable. Reavis was found guilty, sentenced to two years in the federal penitentiary, and fined $5,000. Sofia sought a divorce, moved to Denver, and became a milliner to support their sons. Reavis died penniless in 1914 after several other confidence games failed, never admitting his monumental hoax.

CHAPTER FIFTEEN

Al Sieber

*Al Sieber lived for the action of scouting
and battle. A German immigrant and
Civil War veteran, he ended up in Arizona
leading General George Crook's elite
Apache scouts through 15 years of the most
dangerous fighting of the Indian wars.*

BY LEO W. BANKS

—————

A WRITER ONCE DESCRIBED AL SIEBER, THE U.S ARMY'S chief of scouts during the Apache wars, as "a man of blood and iron, a hardened human instrument employed by civilization to execute its most terrible edicts."

Those words, written by Frank Lockwood in 1934, probably didn't go far enough. Sieber was all of that and more, a tracker, sharpshooter, and fighter without parallel, who, by one estimate, suffered 28 bullet and arrow wounds.

But his most remarkable feat was his day-to-day command of the scouts, the literally wild men that he led, sometimes through some of the most difficult fighting the West ever knew.

Dan Thrapp, Sieber's biographer, wrote that no one else could have done what Sieber did for more than 15 years. He controlled his scouts completely.

An interviewer once asked Sieber to account for the

eerie hold he maintained over his Apaches, and his response is vivid testimony about the man and his times:

"I do not deceive them, but always tell them the truth. When I tell them I'm going to kill them, I do it, and when I tell them I am their friend, they know it."

Sieber was born near Heidelberg, Germany, on February 29, 1844. As a young boy his family emigrated to the United States, living at Lancaster, Pennsylvania, for a time, then Minnesota.

At 18, Sieber enlisted in the Union Army and suffered serious head and leg wounds at Gettysburg. When the war ended he headed west and tried his hand at mining, eventually landing in San Bernardino, California, where he found work herding horses to Prescott, Arizona.

He arrived there about 1868. He was 24. In his pocket he carried the full fruits of his mining labors, about 50 cents. But money never made him jump. Packing, scouting, and warfare did.

Sieber got his first taste of Indian fighting as a wood cutter and ranch foreman in the Williamson Valley, near Prescott. He organized parties of whites to pursue marauding Indians, and his success attracted the army's attention.

When Gen. George Crook came to the territory to fight Indians, he put Sieber in charge of a large party of Apache scouts.

Beginning with his posting at Fort Verde in 1873, and continuing for 13 years, Sieber was in the field almost constantly, sometimes for weeks at a time, "the only white man with thirty to one hundred scouts," noted writer Dan Williamson, a friend of Sieber's.

He lived day after day in constant danger of assassination by disgruntled scouts. Thrapp called it the "most eminently hazardous post held by any white man in the Southwest."

It was an extraordinary period. Sieber was repeatedly called upon to hunt down and kill renegades, destroy their *rancherias*, prevent runaway bands from escaping across the border, and even ride into Mexico to spy on hostile encampments.

His bravery was conspicuous. Lt. Britton Davis, one of those who fought with him, wrote, "If there was ever a man who actually did not know physical fear, that man was Al Sieber."

That courage was never more evident than in 1875 when the army herded almost 1,500 Tonto Apaches and other Indians from Camp Verde to San Carlos, a distance of 180 miles. Without Sieber, the arduous expedition almost certainly would've failed.

While en route, warring bands of Tontos and other Apaches squared off in a gun battle atop a mesa. With several warriors already dead or wounded, it seemed likely that a massacre would unfold. But Sieber ran onto the mesa amid a hail of Indian bullets, and by the sheer force of his will stopped it.

Thrapp wrote that Sieber knew "no finer moment than when he stood between the imprisoned, furiously shooting braves of these great Indian nations, his arms upraised, his blazing eyes literally cowing them into ceasing fire without he himself firing a shot."

But he did plenty of shooting at the Battle of Big Dry Wash atop the Mogollon Rim at Chevelon's Fork in 1882. In recollections on file at the Arizona Historical Society, then 2nd Lt. Thomas Cruse recalls holding the left flank of the Army's position with Sieber at his side.

". . . I heard Al's gun go off, and saw an Indian suddenly rise from a crouching position, throw up his arms and roll over the brink of the canyon. This was repeated three times . . . . I could not see one of these Indians until Al had brought him down."

Every time one of the Apaches plunged off into the canyon, Sieber muttered, "There he goes."

When Cruse decided to charge the Apache position, Sieber warned him to stay put, saying there were still too many Indians. Cruse charged anyway, and quickly learned that Sieber was right.

But the chief of scouts and his men laid down a withering fire that probably saved Cruse, who later won the Congressional Medal of Honor for his action. "It might've been a different tale had not Sieber been there and covered our advance," Cruse wrote.

Not all Sieber's exploits have a heroic hue. He wasn't by temperament a brutal man, but he was a creation of the frontier and a product of war. In Thrapp's words, that meant he could be "kind and murderous and gentle and firm in rapid succession."

If maintaining discipline required summary executions,

he performed them, sometimes shooting down a rebellious scout in the presence of his companions.

Lt. Britton Davis, author of *The Truth about Geronimo*, wrote of an incident involving a renegade captured while on a long scout. Rations were low, and the troop was a considerable distance from any resupply.

The commander lamented having to feed and guard the prisoner until they returned to post. Sieber stepped in. The captive had just finished breakfast and was smoking a cigarette by the campfire when Sieber walked up behind him and shot him through the head.

A trooper sitting nearby watched the body pitch forward into the fire and said, "Say, Al, if you were going to do that, why in hell didn't you do it before he got his belly full of grub?"

Wrote Davis: "Such was the callousness with which the white man had come to regard the taking of the red man's life. Exasperated, our senses blunted by Indian atrocities, we hunted them and killed them as we hunted and killed wolves."

Sieber's control over his Apaches even included performing marriage ceremonies for them. Col. William H. Corbusier, an Army surgeon, recalled what happened when Sieber returned to Camp Verde with captured Indian women. The women were asked where they wished to go, and about 50 crossed to where Sieber's scouts stood.

The scouts wanted the women, too. "Al Sieber then explained that he was going to marry them in the white man's way and they must always remain faithful," Corbusier wrote. "He then told the couples to join hands and he pronounced them man and wife. All left apparently happy."

Remarkably, Sieber's scouts rarely showed resentment at his iron rule. They feared and respected him. And they held him in awe because only the most hardened Apache could stay with him on the trail.

Whites in the territory came to revere him as well. In 1892, the *Arizona Enterprise* wrote that "his name is sacred to the early pioneers, many of whom are indebted to him for the preservation of their scalp locks."

Sieber never married and, according to his biographer, never loved. But he wasn't a loner. He was partial to poker, whiskey, and trading yarns with close friends. He never boasted, allowing Army officers, some of whom couldn't tote his Henry rifle, to take credit for successes he alone engineered.

He once was photographed wearing an ostentatious buckskin suit, probably made for him by an Apache squaw. But he considered the picture embarrassing and never wore the outfit again.

Lockwood said Sieber had "a hand like an elephant." He stood five-feet-10-inches tall, weighed 170 pounds, and had sharp gray eyes that made him an uncanny marksman. He once took aim at a zigzagging jackrabbit from the cab of a bouncing stagecoach and dropped it with a single shot.

The two great failures of Sieber's life came late in his career. The first was in May, 1885, when Davis sent a wire to San Carlos asking for help in quelling a disturbance at the Indian encampment at Fort Apache.

Capt. Francis Pierce, a newcomer to the command, hurried to Sieber's side asking what to do. Awakened from a night of boozing, and still feeling its effects, the old scout told Pierce to ignore Davis' plea.

"Oh, it's nothing but a *tizwin* (a beer-like corn

beverage) drunk," he said. "Davis will handle it." It was a disastrous mistake that led directly to the outbreak of 144 Apaches, including Geronimo.

The second failure occurred June 1, 1887, when Sieber was shot in the leg at San Carlos while trying to arrest the Apache Kid, one of his scouts. The incident was a bitter one for Sieber. He narrowly escaped amputation, and, in spite of a secret government fund given to him to capture the renegade, the Kid was never found.

In December, 1890, after a personal dispute with the commander at San Carlos, Sieber was fired. "I have nothing more to do with the Indians and am clade [sic] of it," the old scout wrote to a friend in his fractured English.

Sieber spent his last years working mining claims around Globe and trying to avoid the writers who kept hounding him for interviews.

The noted Prescott historian Sharlot Hall finally convinced Sieber to talk. Their plan was to take a horseback journey to the scenes of his many exploits in Arizona and Sonora. The resulting interview would've yielded a bonanza of tales about the Apache wars.

But the trip never came off. On February 19, 1907, while supervising Indian laborers on a road-building crew near Roosevelt Dam, a boulder rolled off a slope and crushed Sieber to death.

His body was taken to Globe and draped in a silken, gold-tasseled American flag. Mourning was great, especially among Apaches. "There was weeping among the older Indians from San Carlos to Fort Apache," wrote Williamson in 1931.

Sieber was eulogized as the greatest scout of them all, a man who, in Britton Davis' view, repeatedly risked his life to save others. He was buried in the cemetery at Globe, beneath a marker purchased by the territorial legislature.

But the great scout got a second monument as well, built by his Apache laborers. It still stands near the site of his death, about a mile from the dam.

In his biography, Thrapp noted the widespread rumors that Sieber's death was in fact murder, committed by Apaches with a grudge. It might've been so. But the question of whether the boulder was shoved or fell has remained unanswered.

In a way the ambiguity of Sieber's death fits that of his life. He was a hard man who performed a brutal job during a bloody time, a killer or savior, depending on the moment.

Joseph Rutherford Walker

He lived to travel and see new and wild country.
Throughout the middle 1800s he wandered
the West as a mountain man, explorer, and guide
for emigrants, surveyors, and prospectors.
On his last great expedition 62-year-old
Joe Walker led more than 20 men through
the wilds of Arizona and New Mexico to discover
the rich gold strike that spawned Prescott,
capital of Arizona Territory.

B Y   D A V I D   L A V E N D E R

———

T HE LOST-MINE STORY THAT JACK RALSTON TOLD GEORGE Lount in 1858 ran true to form. Twenty years before, during the winter of 1837-38, Ralston had been wandering through the mountains of what became Arizona with a band of beaver hunters led by the famed mountain man Joseph Rutherford Walker.

One dark night, parched with thirst, the explorers came to the gorge of the Little Colorado River. While some of them groped a risky way down into the canyon, Ralston stayed on top with their horses. Idly he picked up a few pebbles containing bright metallic spots. He pocketed them but made no effort to learn anything about them. Eventually he lost them. Twenty years later, on encountering George

Lount working a prospect in southern Oregon, he remembered.

"Gold! Hell's fire, George, I know where we can pick up mule loads of rock like that!"

They put together a party to go to the Little Colorado, which in 1858 was still in the heart of no-man's-land. The ill-prepared effort aborted in the deserts of southeastern California. Before they could regroup, Ralston fell mortally ill. He did manage, however, to urge Lount to visit Joe Walker on the old trapper's California cattle ranch. Joe's memory for geography and his skill in traversing unmapped lands were legendary. He'd get Lount to the place of the pebbles. Just give him a chance.

Joseph R. Walker. A journalist preparing an obituary of the renowned explorer in 1876 asked a family member what the "R" stood for. Almost surely, Bil Gilbert speculates in his biography of Walker, *Westering Man*, the relative responded "Rutherford," a common name among the Walkers. But the journalist, writing phonetically, came out with "Reddeford." For some reason — perhaps "Rutherford" sounded too high-toned for such a man — the misnomer stuck.

He was something to see, as we know from a picture Alfred Jacob Miller painted of him at the slam-bang Green River fur-trade rendezvous of 1837, the year Jack Ralston fell in with him. Walker was then 38 years old, having been born in Tennessee on December 13, 1798. His 6-foot frame weighed more than 200 hard-conditioned pounds. His buckskin clothes were garnished with Indian finery made by one of the women with whom he consorted during those years. A glossy black beard covered most of an unexpectedly gentle countenance.

His deeds were as striking as his appearance. He was one of the first American traders to reach New Mexico over the Santa Fe Trail. He was the first sheriff of Jackson County, Missouri, then the take-off point for the West. While leading a brigade of trappers in 1833, he became the first white man to see Yosemite Valley and its nearby groves of giant redwood trees. He guided emigrant parties to Oregon and gold-hungry forty-niners to California. During the 1850s, he hunted for a practical wagon road across central New Mexico, which in those days embraced Arizona; his thought was that one day the route might do for a railroad.

Although he often guided miners, he never mined. Grubbing in the ground was too confining. He wanted space. His great love was exploration, particularly in the wild, rumpled rectangle of land that lies between the Colorado River on the north and the Gila River on the south — the heart of today's Arizona.

When prospector George Lount finally located him on his California ranch in the spring of 1861, Walker's hair and beard were turning thin and white. The glasses he wore hinted at failing eyesight. But he looked as sturdy as ever. He said he remembered the place on the Little Colorado where Ralston had picked up the pebbles. Gold? Joe was indifferent about that. But he was 62 years old that year, and this might be his last chance to lead another major trip through deserts and mountains still largely unknown. Yes, he said. He'd go.

Unmindful of the Civil War that had recently erupted in the East, the two men put together a party of 20 or more well-armed prospectors. When the approach of winter brought cool weather, they crossed the main Colorado

River with their string of pack mules and aimed east toward the San Francisco Peaks. Snow was mantling the high country when they reached their destination.

Disappointment flooded them. A thorough combing of the lava-capped ground unearthed no nuggets like those described by Jack Ralston. As the more experienced members of the party belatedly pointed out, gold seldom existed in formations such as those through which the Little Colorado clawed its rugged way below its great falls. Ralston must have been fooled by iron pyrites or stains of copper.

The discouraged men looked at Walker. What now?

Joe felt vaguely guilty. He was supposed to be an expert on the geography of the West, but because he had never been interested in mining, he had not learned to recognize the kinds of geologic formations that were likely to bear metals. True, he'd done what he'd promised; he'd brought the people to the Little Colorado.

Still, he felt he should make amends of some sort for the barren trip. So he told the men of granite mountains off to the southwest where minerals might exist. Just that lifted their spirits. But he brought them back to earth. Before they could undertake as extensive a search as that, they would have to ride east to Albuquerque and replenish their supplies.

At Albuquerque, where they arrived early in 1862, the Civil War caught up with them. Confederates from Texas were sweeping up the Rio Grande, toppling the federal forts that stood in their way. Having no desire to be conscripted to fight for either side, most of the Walker party turned away from the battlefields and crossed snowy Raton Pass into Colorado. There they made their way to newly discovered diggings in the mountains back of Denver. They might find what they wanted there — and Walker might learn enough about gold-bearing formations to pinpoint likely spots he had unwittingly traversed during earlier trips in what is now Arizona.

The steam quickly went out of the Confederate invasion. Colorado volunteers defeated the Southerners at Glorietta Pass east of Santa Fe. Shortly thereafter Col. (later Brig. Gen.) James H. Carleton led a large force of Californians into the Rio Grande Valley. Setting up headquarters at Santa Fe, he placed New Mexico, and therefore Arizona as well, under martial law while he launched a relentless campaign against the Indians of the Southwest. It was the Indians' hope that the whites were so disorganized by their struggle with each other that both tribes of them, Unionists and Confederates, could be driven out of the region.

Joseph Walker, bored with sitting around the fading Colorado goldfields, followed military developments with keen interest. He knew Carleton from the days he had helped Army units find their way around the West. And in Colorado he had learned enough about ore bodies that he felt he could go straight to productive regions in the granitic mountains that lay, as he had told his prospectors, southwest of the great falls of the Little Colorado. All he needed, he believed, was a pass from Carleton and a strong enough party to defend itself against the Apaches.

The probability of running into Apaches cooled the ardor of several of the original party. George Lount and a few others, however, had faith enough in Walker to accompany him. In Colorado and New Mexico they added more recruits, bringing the strength of the party to about 35 men. Carleton granted Walker permission to enter the otherwise restricted area, probably because the guide hinted strongly to the general that he was sure he could locate gold in the forbidden area. That stirred Carleton. One of his aims in quelling the Indians was opening the Southwest to prospecting.

Hoping to break safely through the cordon of Apaches guarding the passes through the Continental Divide, some of Walker's hard-case miners managed to seize the great chief of the Mimbreños, Mangas Coloradas (Red Sleeves) as a hostage. Unhappily a detachment of American soldiers arrived at that inopportune moment and demanded that the chief be turned over to them. That night his guards killed him because, so they reported untruthfully, Mangas was trying to escape.

While the demoralized Mimbreños were skirmishing with the troopers, Walker's party zigzagged swiftly through the mountains with only minor trouble. After passing through Tucson, they turned north to the traditionally friendly villages of the Pima Indians, located a few miles south and west of the site of modern Phoenix. As usual, a few Americans, Mexicans, and mixed bloods were hanging around with the Indians. To this group Walker's people announced loudly and often that they were planning a prospecting expedition to unnamed but promising mountains. They would return to the villages in a month or so to announce results. Quite clearly the miners were fishing for an audience — a big audience. This in turn means that they were counting strongly on Walker's guidance.

Having spread the word, they made their way across desolate wastelands to the mouth of the generally dry Hassayampa River. Toiling up that stream, they came at last to the collection of high, cool, pine-scented, granite-bound peaks and ridges that give birth to the headwater tributaries of the river. Walker had been there years before without knowing what lay under his feet. Six months in Colorado, however, had sharpened his perceptions. Following his directions, his prospectors scattered out among the mountain brooks — Lynx, Big Bug, Turkey, and other creeks hitherto unnamed. Quickly they proved him right. Placer gold — lots of it, they told each other.

Under the tutelage of the California and Colorado hands in the party, they stopped work long enough to form what they called the Walker Mining District. With very little argument, they drew up stringent regulations about the filing of claims — regulations that clearly favored their own interests. Then back to the Pima Villages they went, heedless of the heat of late May, 1863, to record their claims. That done and the claims secure, they broadcast word of their discoveries to the hopefuls who had assembled there, awaiting the report they had been promised. Walker and another friend of Carleton's also sent letters and samples of the Hassayampa gold to the general in Santa Fe.

Their motives are plain. As old hands at the prospecting game, they had learned that, in general, the best way to profit from a mineral claim, once you owned it, was not to mine it but create the excitement and sell it to a latecomer.

They succeeded better than they anticipated. Carleton was ecstatic. He wrote his military superiors; he wrote the postmaster general in Washington. "Our country," he declared, "has mines of precious metals, unsurpassed in richness, numbers, and extent than any in the world." Build forts and roads, he urged. Establish post offices. Create a new government center — for President Lincoln had recently signed a bill splitting Arizona away from New Mexico as a territory unto itself.

The new territorial officials reached the gold camp, population 1,000, in January, 1864. The overnight town soon would be named Prescott. On arriving there, the new governor, John Goodwin, declared that Prescott, not Tucson as originally chosen, was to be the territorial capital.

For a little while the town kept up its merry dance. When the placer mines began to play out, the developers launched a new craze, fling claims on subsurface quartz veins and then selling those to a continuing stream of newcomers. Records show that Joseph R. Walker did file on a quartz claim, though whether he made money on it is unknown. Mostly he preferred taking long trips through the countryside with a young friend, Daniel Conner, who had joined the party in Colorado.

In 1867 the quartz boom also faded, and the capital was shifted to the original choice, Tucson. (It would return temporarily to Prescott during a second boom 10 years later.) By coincidence, Walker's eyes had failed to such a condition by 1867 that he had difficulty getting around. Rather than burden others, he left the town for whose existence he had been responsible and settled on a nephew's ranch in California. Nine years later, totally blind, he died. No man had done more to open the West or had stored up more memories, especially of the wildly beautiful parts of central Arizona, than he had. That was the gold Joe Walker had found for himself.

Arizona As Only *Arizona*

Tucson To Tombstone
In this guidebook, avid southeastern Arizona explorer Tom Dollar tells stories of the region and takes you over its trails. As you learn facts and legends of the Old West, you'll travel from desert floor to riparian canyons to alpine forests. Features maps, travel tips, and more than 128 full-color photographs. Softcover. 96 pages.
#ATTS6 $12.95

Arizona Ghost Towns and Mining Camps
Ghost town authority Philip Varney brings the Old West to life with captivating anecdotes and a gallery of rare, historic photographs. Regional maps, detailed travel information, and a full-color photographic portfolio tell what each site is like today and make this fascinating history of Arizona's mining boom a reliable travel guide as well. Softcover. 136 pages. **#AZGS4 $14.95**

We Call It "Preskit"
Explore the frontier history and hometown charm of Prescott and the high country of central Arizona with author Jack August. The full-color book features things to see and do in the area, including Jerome. Softcover. 64 Pages. **#APRS6 $12.95**

Cow Pie Ain't No Dish You Take to the County Fair
That's just one of the cowboy witticisms in *Arizona Highways'* first humor book. Accompanied by Western cartoonist Jim Willoughby's whimsical illustrations, this collection of 165 jokes, riddles, and one-liners takes a fun and friendly look at the simple facts of cowboy life. You'll laugh out loud. Softcover. 144 pages. **#ACWP7 $6.95**

Highways Can Present It

Manhunts & Massacres
Pieced together from the annals of Arizona's frontier days, here are 18 stories recounting cleverly staged ambushes, massacres that cried out for justice, and the valiant, sometimes vicious, pursuits staged by lawmen and Indian fighters. Softcover. 144 pages.
#AMMP7 $7.95

Days Of Destiny
This book features 20 historical stories about Arizona's worst desperados, the lawmen who brought them to justice, and how Fate changed their lives. Gathered by *Arizona Highways* from more than 70 years of writing about the Old West. Softcover. 144 pages.
#ADAP6 $7.95

Law Of The Gun
Historian and author Marshall Trimble presents an overview of those who wielded the gun to break the law, those who embraced the gun to uphold it, and the guns they used. You'll marvel at the stories of such compelling figures as Wyatt Earp, Wild Bill Hickok, John Wesley Hardin, Jesse James, the Daltons, and Judge Roy Bean. Includes 20 historic photos. Softcover. 192 pages.
#AGNP7 $8.95

They Left Their Mark: Heroes and Rogues of Arizona History
These larger-than-life characters have boldly written their names on the pages of Arizona history. From the early Spanish explorer Juan Bautista de Anza to land swindler James Addison Reavis to World War II Marine hero Ira Hayes, *They Left Their Mark* presents fascinating biographies of Arizona's famous and infamous. Softcover. 144 pages.
#ATMP7 $7.95